To all who have served and loved St. Mary's in the last century and a half, this book is dedicated.

The Tartan Kirkie:

150 years of St. Mary's Episcopal Church, Aberdeen

N.J. Mills

CONTENTS

ACKNOWLEDGMENTS

Thanks to Ruaraidh Wishart of Aberdeen City Archives, June Ellner, Mary Sabiston and Kim Downie of Aberdeen University Special Collections, and Stuart Donald of Aberdeen & Orkney Diocesan Archive.

The cover photograph is by Mike Kenny.

Very many thanks to all at St. Mary's who have contributed help, reminiscences and photographs to this book, and to those who took the time to read, correct and comment on the text before publication. Any mistakes are the author's own.

Chapter One

The Foundations

THE CHURCH OF SAINT MARY'S
CARDEN PLACE, ABERDEEN

There will be Sold, by Public Auction, within the ROYAL
HOTEL,
Union Street, Aberdeen, upon THURSDAY the 10th day of
November, 1864, at Two o'clock Afternoon precisely,

ALL and WHOLE That PIECE of GROUND,
measuring 1 rood 22 poles and 1 ¾ yards imperial measure,
lying on the South Side of CARDEN PLACE, Skene Street,
Aber-
deen, with the BUILDING thereon, known as SAINT MARY'S
CHURCH.

This Church is well known as a new and

beautiful Structure, erected at great cost, and
finished with much taste and elegance. It was
built for an Episcopal Congregation, who now use
it, but with slight alterations in the interior, it
might be adapted for a Congregation of any other
Communion. The Purchase of the Church will
include the valuable Organ, and the whole
Fittings and Furnishings now within the Church,
so far as belonging to the Assignee for the
Creditors of the Rev. Mr. Lee.

Upset price, £3800 sterling

In 1857, Bishop William Skinner, son of the famous John
Skinner of Longside and consolidator of the Scottish Episcopal
Church, Bishop of Aberdeen since 1816, died.

There were two candidates for the vacant see: Dr. Suther of
St. Andrew's Church, King Street, and the Rev. Patrick Cheyne of St.
John's Church, Crown Street. It was a competition between two sides
in a battle that was causing rifts in the Church of England, and it
would very quickly have serious effects in Scotland, and particularly
in Aberdeen.

The Oxford Movement arose in the 1830s and 1840s
amongst certain Oxford-related clerics, including John Henry
Newman, Edward Bouverie Pusey, and Richard Hurrell Froude, who
felt that the Reformation, from the foundation of the Church of
England in the sixteenth century, had gone too far and was
abandoning its Catholic roots. With a particular influence on
architecture and church decoration, the Movement promoted ritual,
vestments, and certain doctrinal reforms which would affect the way
people attended church services. Patrick Cheyne, along with many
Scottish Anglicans, had been strongly influenced by the Oxford
Movement, but Thomas Suther was strongly opposed to it.

Dr. Suther was elected by a small majority, and consecrated in
Edinburgh. In the following March, Patrick Cheyne published his 'Six
Sermons on the Doctrine of the Most Holy Eucharist'

in which he maintained the doctrine of the real presence in the Communion elements, and the cognate doctrines of the identity of the Eucharistic sacrifice with the sacrifice of the Cross, the adoration of the elements, the sufficiency of priestly communion, &c.

The Tablet, 11th. December 1858

This publication was taken to Bishop Suther, who was not noted in the early years of his episcopate for cool and calm relationships with his clergy. Cheyne had been the incumbent at St. John's since 1818: he would not defend himself in the face of Suther's accusations, and was deprived of his office.

The congregation at St. John's had no power to overthrow Bishop Suther's decision. Instead, they showed their feelings by inviting as Cheyne's successor a young man from London who had staunchly defended Cheyne. Frederick George Lee was minister of Berkeley Chapel, a small proprietary chapel in the fashionable parish of St. George's, Hanover Square. Lee was at first reluctant to accept, but finally wrote to St. John's vestry in January 1860:

I feel quite confident moreover that at the expiration of three years you will not fail to recollect that as I have given up all hopes of preferment in the Church in which I was ordained, and have thrown in my lot with her Scotch sister, at a time when the position of the latter was neither satisfactory nor the future very certain, you will not be unwilling as representing the Congregation to give me as far as possible both that pecuniary and moral support which the post I occupy so greatly stands in need of. On my part I can truly say that I will strive to make our future path smooth: though at no sacrifice of principle or compromise of truth.

Minutes of St. John's Episcopal Church, Crown Terrace

The last sentence must have rung rather hollow very quickly, for Lee was determined to impose his Oxford Movement beliefs on

St. John's. He was particularly offended at the fact that many of the congregation attending a Communion service would leave after the sermon, before the Communion. Early in 1861, he preached a sermon on the irregularity of that custom. The next morning he was accosted in the vestry by a member of the congregation who, with his wife and sister, accused the Rector of preaching directly at them. This was the beginning of a series of disputes between Lee and the congregation and he decided to resign. A vestry meeting was called, at which twenty-seven to twelve members voted in favour of the Rector. Lee was wavering when 285 members of the congregation sent to the Rector a spontaneous resolution that, if he were to resign, they would follow and form a new congregation with him as incumbent, with the Bishop's consent. Lee resigned, with mixed feelings – he sent this letter to the churchwardens, George Grub and Dr. George Ogilvie:

> As I shall shortly address a Public Letter to you and to the congregation generally, I need only add that I thank you for the uniform kindness and consideration with which you have treated me since I came to Scotland – merely forgetting the proceedings of Thursday – and with an earnest hope that my successor may be more successful than it has been my lot to be in labouring amongst you.
>
> Minutes of St. John's Episcopal Church, Crown Terrace

Lee was replaced by John Comper, whose contribution to the church life of Aberdeen has been widely recognised. Premises were found for Lee and his faithful followers in the Old Writing School in Correction Wynd, which had formerly been a Baptist Chapel, and there Lee was free to establish a place of worship fully in line with his Oxford Movement ideals. Two years later, waiting for their new church building to be completed, the congregation was joined by a correspondent for the *Church Times*, who reported in detail on his experience.

> I was staying a short distance from Aberdeen, and on All Saints' Eve I made inquiries whether there would be any services, and ascertained that Evensong

would be sung at St. Mary's Mission Chapel at 8.15p.m. With some difficulty I found my way there. The first appearance of the chapel was not very pleasing, as it had the usual barn-like appearance of places where Dissenters love to congregate (once a week). It was, I believe, formerly a Baptist conventicle, and was bought by the Mission for temporary use until they could build a church.

A glance, however, at the east end convinced me that I was in a Catholic place of worship. A correctly shaped altar vested for the festival, cloth of gold frontal, white lace superfrontal; on super-altar a jewelled cross, with two sacramental candles (unlighted), vases of flowers, and four large many-branched candlesticks, with lights burning, a crimson dorsal cloth, a painting hung on it of the Blessed Virgin and Holy Child. ... the altar [was] censed during Magnificat.

The whole congregation remained throughout until the last benediction.

The celebrant was vested in an alb (stole crossed) and chasuble with a large cross on the back of it. The deacon and subdeacon were in albs, stole and tippets; the lay clerks and choir men in cottas and tippets; the acolytes in short muslin cottas, reaching to the waist. Of course every one wore cassocks; the priests carried berettas in their hands ...

I have no hesitation in saying that at no church in London are the congregation so attentive or devout, or the services conducted with greater reverence than at this little mission chapel, in the midst of heretics and schismatics.

I sincerely believe that the opening of the new church of St. Mary's ... will be under God, the beginning of the end of Protestantism in Aberdeen ...

Church Times, November 14th., 1863

Meanwhile, Lee had found and purchased land in the west end of Aberdeen not far from his house, and the foundation stone for his new church was laid by Bishop Suther. However, the Bishop's sympathy was short-lived: when he saw the completed building in 1864, he refused to licence it until several changes were made. Specifically, he demanded the removal of the figures of Jesus, St. John and Mary from the rood beam, together with the sanctuary lamp, and he wanted a written guarantee that the altar in the crypt chapel would not be used for a celebration of Holy Communion. He also insisted that Lee abandon the use of vestments and incense.

A possible Cathedral

When the building of St. Mary's was in contemplation in 1861, Aberdeen still lacked an Episcopal cathedral. The matter was under debate, when a letter was printed, addressed to the Bishop, Thomas Suther. It was from George J.R. Gordon, Esq., younger of Ellon, H.M. Envoy Extraordinary and Minister Plenipotentiary to the King of Wurtemberg, etc., and was sent from Stuttgart, August 1861.

George Gordon wrote an eight page letter arguing that the current ideas for an Aberdeen cathedral were unsatisfactory. 'St. Andrew's', he declared, 'is too small', and has an 'insufficient and incorrect ecclesiological plan', and St. John's is too small and 'does not possess architecturally the necessary dignity of character'!

Instead, Gordon wanted the new church planned for Carden Place to be the new Aberdeen Cathedral. He wanted it to be a cathedral for everyone, not just F.G. Lee's rebel church. He suggested fundraising from London and America, from nobles and lairds, from tenant farmers and from the poor.

What would the West End of Aberdeen be like if the Diocese had agreed with the plan?

Lee protested but Suther stood firm, maintaining that St. Mary's was contravening the laws of the Episcopal Church by not being in communion with St. John's. Lee took legal advice, the result being that the opening service in March, 1864, set up St. Mary's as a proprietary chapel only. It may have galled Bishop Suther that it was attended by seven to eight hundred people with a choir of fifty-five, and various clergy from as far afield as London.

The battle lines were drawn up: Lee refused to close the church and Suther refused to licence or consecrate it, and there it may have stayed but that Lee had gravely overreached himself financially in the building of St. Mary's, became bankrupt, and fled to London. The auction of the entire contents of his house was announced in the *Aberdeen Journal* of 11th. October, right down to the fenders, fireirons and crib, and including a telescope table. The valuable library and paintings were to be sold separately later. Then on the following day the church itself was advertised for sale, complete with the organ. The auction for the church was to be on 10th. November, but the creditors changed their minds and other solutions were sought.

The congregation wanted to replace Lee with Thomas Dove Dove, another High Churchman. Churchwardens were appointed, Thomas Gordon Beveridge and William Fraser, and two advocates were nominated as arbiters between the church and the Bishop, and discussions continued. They culminated in a Synod held at Perth in July 1865, a poorly attended and rather unseemly debate between Bishop Suther and the representatives of St. Mary's, which was fully reported over four pages in the *Scottish Guardian*.

> The Bishop established St. Mary's as a Mission; raised it to an incumbency; attended services at the temporary Church; encouraged the faithful to contribute to the new Church by his Episcopal recommendation; sanctioned the foundation of the Church by his presence; approved of the solemn form for its opening; and then drew back, on the eve of its completion, on account of certain objections – all of which, so far as the building is concerned, have been conceded.

> The appellants, after having read their reasons, declined to make any further remarks at that time, and the Bishop replied that he had no intention to enter into the merits of the case. He had two legal reasons for this – First, he denied the competency of

the appellants, and second, he denied the competency of the College of Bishops to hear this appeal ...

[The Bishop] had encouraged St. Mary's, because he believed he was dealing with conscientious gentlemen, but in this he was deceived ...

Mr. Beveridge ... conceived that they had a great grievance to complain of. The Bishop of Aberdeen had spoken of their disobedience. They had not disobeyed in any single instance. Whenever they had applied to be heard, they had been met with the complaint of their being schismatical and rebellious. But the Bishop had never stated particulars.

The Bishop of Aberdeen: You knew that I had not licenced the church, yet you went into it, and you continued, despite my authority, to use illegal ornaments.

Mr. Beveridge: I hold these ornaments to be quite lawful according to the Rubric prefixed to the Book of Common Prayer which this Church has recently adopted. But we did not stand upon this. Our Bishop said they were unlawful, and without contesting his authority, we have removed them.

The Bishop argued that the congregation had no rights in the matter as they had no incumbent, no incumbent's warden, and no licenced church, though as the Bishop of Brechin drily pointed out, the Bishop himself had caused all these circumstances of which he was now taking advantage.

The argument was adjourned to the October Synod, which eventually allowed the congregation to continue. Dove and the churchwardens were determined to act like a normal church, even if they were not officially part of the Scottish Episcopal Church. The first minuted congregational meeting was held on 9th. November, 1865, and discussed matters such as how to increase church membership. Dove had been negotiating all year to buy the church building and grounds from Lee's creditors, and the purchasers on behalf of the congregation were to be five lay male communicants over the age of twenty-one, three named by the incumbent and two elected by the congregation, who were also to have the power to elect an incumbent until the church was consecrated. The vestry was to comprise these five men, the incumbent, and one man appointed annually by him. Communicant members were to communicate three times a year and pay for a seat or make other financial contribution, or be choristers, to have a vote.

The first trustees for the congregation were Alexander Forbes Irvine of Drum, John Ramsay of Barra, the Hon. George Fraser Boyle of Cumbrae, Norval Clyne (diocesan registrar), and George Auldjo Jamieson, a chartered accountant in Edinburgh, an Aberdeen man who numbered amongst his clients the Earls of Aberdeen, and amongst his friends Alexander Macdonald of Kepplestone, founder of Aberdeen Art Gallery. Once these trustees were in place, Dove and the churchwardens resigned as arranged (Dove was certainly too High Church for Bishop Suther to tolerate in any case) and the trustees applied once again to the Bishop for a licence.

The *Free Press* stated on 5th. December,

> We are glad to announce that the controversy which has so long existed in regard to this church, and the position of the congregation, is now happily at an end.

The first service was held on Advent Sunday, 3rd. December, with the Primus (not the Bishop, interestingly) officiating. In his sermon, he said that he wished

> to express my earnest and anxious hope, that this Advent Sunday may prove the commencement of many years of cordial union between yourselves, your future ministers, and your Bishop, and that you may mutually strengthen each others' hands in the one great work of winning souls to Christ.

The *Free Press* went on:

> Many of the choir and upwards of 70 in the congregation communicated. ... The Choir numbered 26, and the services were choral, both morning and evening, Tallis and Helmore's music being used. The

anthem on both occasions was from King Solomon's prayer at the dedication of the Temple, viz. 'O Lord, my God, hear Thou the prayer thy servant prayeth.'

As the Primus pronounced the Apostolic Benediction, after evening service, standing on the altar steps, the people kneeling, the effect was very solemn and impressive. The offerings amounted to upwards of £12. The congregation in the forenoon well filled the church, and in the evening the crowd was very great. Every one seemed to be impressed by the whole Services, which were felt to unite the simple beauty and solemn majesty of the Church's glorious Services, when celebrated as they were on this day – harmonising so well with the magnificent church in which they were performed.

In beauty of holiness, with ordered pomp,
Decent and unreproved.

We trust that the future of the Church and Congregation will correspond with this auspicious commencement; and we are certain that if the Services are carried on with the like dignity, decency and order, the result of this day will be most happy. We understand that an Incumbent will soon be appointed; and as it is intended, relying on the Church's Offertory that one half of the sittings will be free, it is believed that many will avail themselves there of the opportunities thus given to worship God according to the ritual of the Book of Common Prayer.

Dove was replaced in 1866 by Henry James Palmer. Palmer was thirty-two and had moved from Cheshire, and though sympathetic to the Oxford Movement he was prepared to compromise: the figures were taken down from the rood beam, the inscription on it was erased, and the sanctuary lamp removed. The use of incense and the parading of banners were stopped, and the crypt was dedicated as St. Machar's Chapel. Services were advertised as follows:

Sundays 1st, 2nd and 4th 8am
1st, 3rd and 5th 11.30am
Mattins 11am
Instruction 3pm
Evensong 6.30pm
Daily, Mattins 8am (Wednesdays 11am)
Evensong 8.15
Holy Communion Wednesdays 8am.

Palmer also found it necessary to reform the behaviour of some of those attending his services, and wrote in the church magazine:

A few words to those who do not belong to our congregation, but who yet attend the services of our Church, may not be out of place here. They are words of welcome, for we love to see in His house all those who appreciate the Church's worship of her King. But we *must* ask those who come to join us in our prayers and praises, to join us too in the manner in which we try to offer them. We *must* ask one and all to be mindful of our Blessed Lord's Presence in the midst of His worshippers – to kneel when we kneel, to stand when we stand; to avoid irreverence of demeanour ...

Palmer also suggested that the church set up a Mission school, but the debt continued to be a problem and in November 1868, seeing no solution, Palmer resigned his incumbency, owed two months' salary. He moved to St. Columba's, Edinburgh, in 1869.

Alfred Rudall became incumbent in 1869: his previous church had been in Cornwall, and the change of air never seemed to agree with him. Even several weeks at Ballater could not mend his ill health, and he resigned in August of the same year. The vestry quickly replaced him with Henry David Jones, a Welshman. Jones removed a few High Church details that Rudall introduced, including candle branches on the rood beam and the Latin scroll below them, to be replaced by an English one 'to be selected by Mr Jones'. He removed green cloths from each side of the chancel arch but replaced them with purple ones 'of a church pattern'. Under his direction, payment for sittings was rationalised: the first two seats on each side were free, the next ten each side were let with chairs at a guinea a sitting, the next five seats in each side and chairs at 15/- each, and all others at 10/- each.

By 1870 an arrangement had been made with Jones that for every £500 of the debt paid off, his stipend should be increased by £50p.a. He was at this point to be paid £200p.a. However, his health too was poor and by 1872 he was having to leave Aberdeen during the winter months, and the following year the vestry recorded his 'regret that unfortunate circumstances had more than once caused them annoyance through the great difficulty of obtaining satisfactory clergymen to take the temporary charge of the church'. In September 1873 J.M. Danson was appointed curate, and Jones resigned shortly afterwards.

The vestry decided to advertise the vacancy, despite Danson's insistence on taking on the incumbency. Sensing possible confrontation, the vestry decided to carry on with advertising but not to ask Danson for the use of the church for meetings. A petition from the congregation asked for Danson to be appointed, so it was decided to have a general meeting to discuss the matter. It was at last concluded that Danson be invited to become incumbent at a salary of £200, though the church could only actually afford £141 and that included a special collection at Easter: there was still a debt of £1,871. However, Danson also received a dividend from the Church Society, which made up the balance.

In April 1874, a Bazaar was proposed to liquidate the debt, and arranged for two days in October 1875: it was advertised over a year ahead. It made £1,000, and by moving money to the debt account from an overdraft account, the foundation debt was paid off.

Under Danson the congregation was growing, income was increasing and expenditure and debt were decreasing. By May 1876, his income (still from various sources) had increased to £300. By April 1878 the congregation numbered 326, with 166 communicants, and around 60 attendants at Sunday School in the afternoon. Danson's salary was reduced to £200, but only because he now received the church's new parsonage rent-free. Nevertheless, the overdraft continued to be a problem. Danson received a letter in April 1878:

Dear Sir,

The Debt upon St. Mary's Church, Aberdeen,
I understand, is now about £720; and when the
balance of the late Major Scott's Donation is received,
and the price of the two large Pictures (the gift of
Lady Crawford) is realized, the amount of the Debt
will probably be reduced to about £500.

I have for some time felt that another effort
should be made to clear off the whole remaining
Debt on St. Mary's; and, as the commencement of
such an effort, I herewith hand you a Deposit Receipt
for the sum of One Hundred Pounds, lodged
yesterday in the Aberdeen Town and County Bank in
your name 'In Trust'; and I am to request that you
will apply the said sum, and all interest which may
accrue thereon, towards the extinction of the Debt on
St. Mary's Church – provided that you and the other
friends of St. Mary's shall, on or before Christmas
Day of next year, 1879, by Special Offertories and
Donations (but not by a Bazaar), raise the sum of
Four Hundred Pounds (or such lesser sum as may
prove sufficient) for the same purpose, viz., the
extinction of the whole of the said Debt.
Yours faithfully,
A Member of St. Mary's.

Even this sum could not be reached – or not without another
bazaar! and Danson left in 1880. He spent a year as incumbent of
Arbroath before returning to Aberdeen as incumbent of St.
Andrew's, King Street, where he remained until his death in 1909,
and was Dean of the Diocese from 1907.

Advertisements were drawn up again and the vestry decided
to say that 'a moderate churchman and good preacher is desired'.
Arthur Fenton Still Hill from Hull was appointed in 1880, aged
twenty-seven. Rev. Arthur Douglas was by then Bishop of Aberdeen,
and Hill was able to restore the use of coloured stoles without
causing trouble. By May 1882 the debt had crept up again to £507

and Hill offered to cut his salary to a total of £200. By October 1883 there was talk of mortgaging the church and parsonage, and of paying Hill towards the arrears on his stipend (with no personal obligations). The vestry meetings were an endless juggling of bonds and mortgages and loans, and they made a decision to cease a guaranteed stipend, just paying the incumbent the surplus and the Easter offertory.

In May 1885 a member of the congregation offered to lend money secured on the parsonage to get rid of the debt. The church was still not consecrated. The Bishop was against the loan as it was just transferring the debt and not clearing it – he felt the congregation could easily do this but instead had reduced the stipend 'to a sum that I really do not like to name'. Hill managed on a very variable salary for six years but left in 1886 to return to England.

On his departure, the vestry appointed the church's first Scottish rector. Rev. Francis William Christie from Dundee accepted the incumbency at £120p.a., and an appeal was set up to pay this, which had been guaranteed for three years, along with the Easter offering, the parsonage and half of any surplus, the other half going towards the debt. Christie declined the first Easter offering, saying it should go to the debt. Not since J.M. Danson had the church had such an energetic clergyman, and it is possible that without Christie there would be no St. Mary's today.

The church's little monthly magazines took on a new, less formal character. Christie was specific and forthright in his requests for donations and for attendance.

> The Hymn Board has arrived – and a very nice one it is ... Christmas Decorations – We again record our gratitude to our helpers within and without our own circle. Their work is very tasteful, and does not err in being overdone; but a few shrubs in pots would have enhanced the effect very much.

Christie was relentless in clearing the debt and encouraging his congregation as a community, and more importantly, he stayed put at St. Mary's, showing his own commitment as an example to others. St. Mary's badly needed the continuity.

With bazaars, sales of work, donations, and other fundraising events, Christie and the vestry whittled the debt down to £186. Then, in December 1889, an odd thing happened.

> The Incumbent intimated that on 5th. December last, he received a box per parcel post with £186 enclosed – in gold – along with an anonymous note stating that the amount was intended to make up the balance required for the purchase of the feu duty on the Church.
>
> Vestry minutes, 16th. December, 1889

The donation was acknowledged in the *Scottish Guardian*, and the event led to the rewriting of the constitution and, finally, the consecration of the church.

This happened on 16th. April, 1890, with H.J. Palmer invited back as the preacher. Lunch was held afterwards at Weir's Rooms, 120, Union Street, at 2/6 a ticket. On the poster, it stated:

> The Congregation are requested not to leave the Church after the sermon, but to remain to the end of the service.

St. Mary's was truly established.

A sign of the times:

The fund-raising Bazaar in 1887 included a pet stall!

The Diocese drew up boundaries for the city's churches in 1913: St. Mary's boundaries ran along Queen's Road to Albyn Place, to Victoria Street, to Thistle Street, to Rose Street, to Esslemont Avenue, to Watson Street, to Cornhill Road, to Elmhill Road and to Cairncry Road. As ever, though, the congregation came from all over the city, probably passing members of other Episcopal churches on their way, heading in the opposite direction. The Episcopal Churches in Aberdeen have never enjoyed a strong parochial structure.

Even the congregational debt was cleared by April 1893, though St. Mary's was still grateful for a donation of £250 from the Walker benefaction, founded by the sisters who had funded the building of St. Mary's Cathedral in Edinburgh. Free Will Offering, a new idea in Scotland, was established in 1923. Just before Christmas in the same year, Canon Christie died suddenly, and a chapter in the church's life ended.

Henry Chapman was appointed, but like other incumbents (the term 'Rector' was only used from 1890, following the pattern of the American churches) he suffered ill health in Aberdeen. He took up a post in Buckinghamshire in July 1927, and was replaced by George Lightfoot. Canon Lightfoot was another steady influence on St. Mary's (though there were technological advances: the first telephone was installed in the Rectory in 1937), but in the early 1940s the church was hit by a triple tragedy: Edith Lightfoot, the Rector's wife, died of lung cancer in 1941, Canon Lightfoot himself died suddenly in June, 1942, and after William Milne had taken up the incumbency (£350p.a. with free house and telephone (except for personal trunk calls)), the church was bombed in 1943.

Canon Milne instituted the War Memorial Chapel for weekday celebrations and services of intercession, and had plans to make a Children's Corner on the other side of the choir. Constitutional changes were in progress, too: in November 1943, the minimum age of constituent members was reduced to 18, and the People's Warden and Lay Representative were now on the vestry. In March 1945 the Vestry awarded the Rector travelling expenses of £10p.a. as an experiment, but after a few months this plan was dropped and the stipend raised instead. The post-war years brought their own challenges: it was hard to find anyone to take up the post of verger, and in 1947 the church was burgled, and the vestry took the decision to lock the building at dusk. The new NHS had a minor impact: traditionally, churches in Aberdeen had collaborated in a Sunday Hospital collection to help fund the Royal Infirmary, but that annual collection was turned over to Bethany House instead, the convent with which St. Mary's had a long association. Further technological advances appeared: in 1953 the first electric washing machine was installed in the Rectory. In 1956, the congregation was asked to contribute to the cost of a car for the new Bishop, Edward

Easson, in a rather unusual Bishop's Appeal. By the end of the year subscriptions were required for the purchase of a car for the Rector, too. Land was bought at the back of the rectory to make a lane, and a Ford Popular was purchased. Authority to drive it was given only to the Rector and, alarmingly, the Vestry.

In 1959, the Bishop suggested that St. Mary's might again have a curate, as lay readers were still not permitted by College of Bishops to administer the sacrament. Kenneth Cole, who had been on the vestry before resigning to attend Edinburgh Theological College, returned to St. Mary's as curate in October 1959. In that year, St. Mary's, along with other Episcopal Churches, adopted that universally recognised mark, the Pisky Pub Sign, officially known as the Shannon Hanging Sign Type A, designed by the Rev. Paddy Shannon, Provost of St. Andrew's Cathedral. Some habits continued as they ever had, though: the House of Bethany did the laundry of the altar linen, and St. Margaret's Convent made the Communion wafers.

Hot Air at the Vestry

A new gas fire was installed in the hall in a cold January, 1955, and the vestry quickly arranged to have their meetings there. The size of the substantial gas bill the next month led to some comments about the comfort of the vestry, but apparently a faulty meter was to blame.

Chapter Two

The Buildings

The Church

The first building in which St. Mary's congregation worshipped, in Correction Wynd, was described in unflattering terms in the *Church Times* of 14th. November, 1863:

> The first appearance of the chapel was not very pleasing, as it had the usual barn-like appearance of places where Dissenters love to congregate (once a week). It was, I believe, formerly a Baptist conventicle, and was bought by the Mission for temporary use until they could build a church.

Correction Wynd, though tucked under the high wall of St. Nicholas' churchyard, was at the heart of the city, and convenient for the poorer part of St. John's congregation who left with Rev. F.G. Lee to found a new church. The Wynd itself was home to the workplaces, at least, of an advocate, a jeweller, a tailor, a vintner, a watchmaker, and also to the Free Melville Church.

Despite its convenience, Lee, a creative man, was not going to be satisfied with this plain building for long, and he quickly acquired land in the west end of Aberdeen for his own design of church. The town was quickly expanding to the west, and Lee's choice may well have been governed only by where land was available and other churches were not already around: though St. James' Church was already at Holburn Junction it was not, at the time, part of the Scottish Episcopal Church. The land was

> ... part of the Estate of Rubislaw lying on the south

21

side of the street leading westward from Skene Street of Aberdeen now called Carden Place and extending backwards at right angles therefrom to the new road or street called Albert Terrace lately made out in continuation of Thistle Street, and Waverly Place ...

General Register of Sasines

and Lee bought it from Sir Alexander Anderson of Rubislaw, advocate and provost of Aberdeen, and landlord of his own house. The purchase was completed on 27th. June, 1862, fifteen months after Lee resigned from St. John's.

Four days after the purchase, the foundation stone was laid on 1st. July, 1862: the official working architect was Alexander Ellis (1830 – 1917), but his job was probably not an easy one.

> Lee was a leading member of the Architectural Society of Oxford and an amateur architect: whether he obtained help directly from George Edmund Street, architect to the Oxford Diocese, who certainly designed the Minton tiles, whether he adapted the competition designs for the Crimea Memorial Church and other polychrome continental Gothic designs of that period, or whether Ellis himself had a large hand in the detailing is unclear, but the commission certainly enlarged Ellis's architectural vocabulary.
>
> *Dictionary of Scottish Architects* (accessed 25/vi/10)

The Oxford Movement, of which Lee was a part, had a deep influence on the Gothic Revival, and such features as polychromatic materials and spirelets were typical of the work of Oxford Movement architects like William White. G.E. Street was later responsible for the interdenominational chapel at Haddo House in Aberdeenshire, which also has Gothic Revival features.

The outline design of St. Mary's was simple: the listing of the building describes it as a 'Single storey, simple medieval-plan gothic church'. The nave measured 95 x 40 feet, the chancel 35 x 25 feet, the organ chamber originally lay to the south and the vestry to the north. The side walls of the nave were 30' tall, and from floor to apex the inside of the building was 60' tall.

The construction materials, however, were what made it stand out. The base was built with red Tyrebagger granite, but thereafter grey granite and red and yellow sandstone were used in stripes which become even more apparent inside the building where various colours of brickwork were also used. It quickly acquired the local nickname of the 'Tartan Kirkie', though the *Illustrated London News* described it at its opening as 'one of the handsomest modern ecclesiastical edifices in Scotland'. While the nave was in many ways much as it is today, there was a baptistry curtained off in the north-west corner, with the font in place there: the reconstruction of the 1950s has now replaced the original form of the chancel and crypt.

We are fortunate to have an engraving of the old chancel and also a description written in a brief history of St. Mary's by E. Lightfoot, son of the Rector who died in 1942.

The glass in the East window unhappily destroyed in 1943 was supplied by Messrs Lavers and Barraud of

Bloomsbury. The central circular light represented Our Blessed Lord in majesty and glory, with the Virgin Mary and St. John the Baptist on either side. Below and around nine saints were depicted: St. Andrew, St. Peter, St. Gregory, St. Augustine of Canterbury, St. Margaret of Scotland, St. Thomas the Martyr, St. Cecilia, St. Agnes, and St. Alban, while the seven small circular lights outside represented scenes from Our Lord's life (1) The Annunciation (2) The Birth (3) The Presentation (4) The Baptism (5) The Crucifixion (6) The Resurrection (7) The Ascension ... The majolica tiles which decorated the East wall were from a design by G.E. Street, FSA ... below the floor of the Chancel was the Crypt originally designed as a Mortuary Chapel, the groined ceiling of which, with its pointed arches, was supported on solid stone pillars several of which had finely carved capitals.

In addition, the church had a small tower, as we can see from this early engraving used to illustrate the article in the *Illustrated London News*:

THE EPISCOPALIAN CHURCH OF ST. MARY, CARDEN PLACE, ABERDEEN.

Ellis not only had the difficulties of working with an amateur colleague, however gifted, but also found that Lee was unable to pay for his services. Unfortunately for Ellis, neither the diocese nor the vestry was in a position to settle Lee's accounts, either. Perhaps in the hope that some money would eventually be forthcoming, Ellis continued to do some work for St. Mary's, and three years after Lee's departure he was submitting

> plans and estimates for enclosing the Church ground by a Dwarf Wall and Railing ... it was necessary that these should be substantial and elegant so as to be in keeping with the Church
>
> Vestry minutes, 23rd. April 1867

By this time, too, the first flaws in Lee's amateur design were becoming clear. The main problem was the tower mentioned above.

> Mr. Ligertwood was directed to obtain a Report on the Tower and Roof, and to Carry out any practical suggestion that might be made to insure the dryness of the interior and freedom from Draughts in the Church.
>
> Vestry minutes, 23rd. April, 1867

> ... the condition of the tower and roof continued to give great Annoyance to the Congregation. Altho' very considerable sums had been laid out upon them in repairs during the last two years still the rain, snow and wind came in ...
>
> Vestry minutes, 18th. August, 1869

The reverberation of the 'spirelet' shook the building and drowned out the service, and reluctantly the vestry decided to take it down and reslate. Nevertheless, the decision did not prevent the vestry airing other ideas for adding to the building: at this time, despite lacking funds, they were actively discussing the possibility of having a stone campanile at the north corner of west gable, and in 1900 they looked over a proposal to build a narthex and baptistry on to the west end of the church.

Instead they turned their attention to more prosaic requirements: new heating was required as early as October 1869. There were several bids and the vestry went for the 'least objectionable in structure, as effectual in operation, and not more costly than the others.' 1,500 feet of hot water pipes were installed, at a cost of £150, and the pipes, if not the system, survived into the 21st. century when they were at last removed.

The business of the vestry continued to involve building and refurbishment and urgent repairs, very much as it does today. In 1884 the roof was found to be leaking where the chancel met the vestry. In 1891 it was discovered that the mosaic tiles in the chancel were lifting and there was a nasty smell. The lime which had been used with chippings to bed down the tiles had not been properly slaked, and gas was escaping: perhaps Lee had tried to cut some corners in his building work to save money. In May 1903 the crypt was being refurbished:

> Capitals, pillars and other stonework washed and cleaned. The brickwork of arched ceiling etc. coated with silicate in two colours as before, the red part lined in black and the cream colour lined in red. The cemented walls coated with silicate of a Caen stone colour lined into blocks with white.

The hall was also being built at this time, the small room now called the Choir Vestry. The architect was Arthur Clyne, son of the advocate Norval Clyne who had been involved at St. John's in the dispute resulting in F.G. Lee's departure. In 1906 for insurance the church building was valued at £2,800, the vestry at £750, and with contents the total amount was £4,500. By 1909, St. Mary's was being described as:

> One of the most picturesque ecclesiastical edifices in Aberdeen ... Internally the edifice is admirably adapted for a stately service.
>
> Alexander Gammie

The Diocese of Aberdeen, however, was still looking for a

cathedral: the letter from George J.R. Gordon, younger of Ellon, published in 1861 (see Chapter One), might have discouraged the adoption of St. Andrew's Church in King Street as the cathedral, but it had not entirely persuaded the diocese that St. Mary's would be appropriate. The idea was not unthinkable: in 1909 a letter was sent by the Cathedral Committee of the Diocese to the vestries of both St. Mary's and St. John's, asking if either would be prepared to hand their building over to be the Cathedral. The Committee would retain the right either to turn the building into a Cathedral or to demolish the building and use the site. The vestry of St. Mary's agreed to consider any definite proposal, and a congregational meeting was called. It came up with eight resolutions which would have to be agreed by the Cathedral building committee before the congregation would agree: first, no building work was to start until enough money had been raised to complete a large enough chancel, nave, etc. to accommodate St. Mary's congregation; second, no part of the present church was to be removed until building was complete; three, there was to be financial provision for any expenses incurred by the congregation; four, at least ten representatives of St. Mary's were to be on the building committee; five, the Rector of St. Mary's was to be the first provost of the Cathedral; six, there were to be financial provisions for his stipend; seven, the Scottish Liturgy was to be used at services; and eight, the Cathedral congregation was to be able to appoint a vestry and act in a manner the same as that under the church's constitution. The financial emphasis of these resolutions is hardly surprising, given St. Mary's history, but the conditions must have been too strict for the Cathedral building committee, and no more was said.

St. Mary's continued to change and develop as the circumstances demanded. The stone cross above the roof of the West Door was blown down in gales in 1912, and the vestry discovered rather to their surprise that it was a whole 3' 9" square. It was replaced by one of Rhynie stone, which was cheaper than the original granite. Around the time of the First World War there was ivy on the walls, and a lawn surrounded the church, very different from today's granite chippings and bare walls. The baptistry was still at the back of the church, too, complete with its door and curtains. Mr. Townend of the Art Gallery, consulted on aesthetic improvements to the church, recommended clearing it away and putting a new font in the centre aisle, then adding a porch to the west end. The vestry duly agreed, establishing a new font in its current central position, and employing William Kelly, who had worked on some aspects of the church before, to design a porch. It was to be paid for by the family of Mr. Alexander who had been a vestry member at his death in late 1925. Kelly, famous for his black Kelly's Cats on Union Bridge, designed a porch in dull red Corrennie granite, but Mr. Alexander's family wanted polished Boddam granite. The vestry, unwilling to lose either funding or architect, suggested a compromise in axed Peterhead granite. Kelly objected and then claimed he had no time to oversee the building of the porch, so the firm of Marshall McKenzie was chosen instead in 1926 and the work was completed.

Today's vestry would recognise the frequent discussions on heating the church, with all the usual problems of warming a very tall building, poorly insulated, for several peak points in the week throughout the year for a number of people sitting fairly still, including a proportion of infirm and elderly. In the 1930s Mr. Botting, a heating engineer, was on the vestry, but the problems were still considerable. In March 1942, there was a general complaint that the heating was not adequate on a Sunday morning perhaps due to problems with stoking the boiler. It was suggested that the verger, Mr Greig, should sleep in the church each Saturday night to oversee the boiler (bed and bedding to be supplied), but this seems not to have been adopted (perhaps the verger was not willing).

All problems with the heating were put into perspective by the bomb which hit St. Mary's on the night of 21st. April, 1943. The terrible damage done chiefly to the chancel and crypt, but also to a lesser extent to the rest of the building, brought a new and powerful factor into the vestry's work: the War Damage Commission of the Board of Trade. The War Damage Commission would pay only for the most plain and functional replacement of 'like for like': the building had to have the same footprint and be built to the same height, but much of the material the vestry would have chosen was either unaffordable or not available in wartime conditions. In May, 1944, the secretary reported that Mervyn Wood, a Glasgow architect, 'had been so impressed by the beauty of St. Mary's that he had requested permission to take measurements and prepare plans for a restored Chancel and Church Hall', but however much they liked his

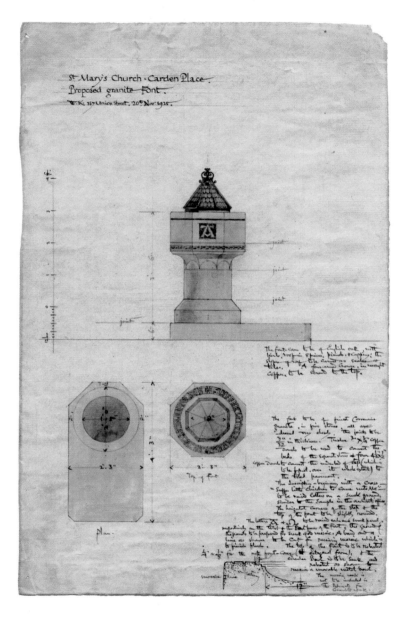

William Kelly's original design for the font: a version with more elaborate stonework but less decoration was eventually selected. This too is in Corrennie granite, with gold and blue mosaic, with a tall oak lid.[1]

---

[1] William Kelly's design: Aberdeen University Library MS3759/A1/14

plan it was unlikely that it could be adopted.

In July 1944 the vestry claimed £1,130-2-4 to replace the furnishings destroyed by the bomb: in general replacing the furnishings seems to have been easier than rebuilding. In May 1945, with the end of the war in sight, the vestry told the War Damage Commission that the east window should be incorporated into the new chancel design and the crypt should be rebuilt, though they agreed to dispense with pillars in the crypt in favour of a more modern type of support. 'Plain repair' was the mantra of the W.D.C., with the rest to be funded by the church: as usual this meant that little could be done. In August of that year a new church hall was proposed as part of the rebuilding work, with new sanitary and kitchen arrangements and swapping the positions of the organ and the sacristy. Only the last part of this could be adopted: the new hall was again shelved. It did not help in the whole restoration that the original plans of church could not be found.

The Government in June 1947 announced its allocation of a sum of £1m for the repair and rebuilding of churches. St. Mary's vestry decided to ask for £10,000 from the £200,000 portion of the pot set aside for repairs. At the same time, Jenkins & Marr, the engineers overseeing the repairs, had their designs dismissed by the W.D.C. as not suitable for 'plain repair'. 'Plain repair', however, the W.D.C. conceded, did include the rose window, piscina, sedilia and high altar and sacristy. Jenkins & Marr dropped out in October, and Major A. Ross, Inverness, took over as architect. He does not appear in the *Dictionary of Scottish Architects*, though he may be the Alexander Ross who appears in the Post Office Directory for that year as a 'designer' in Leslie Road. Architects were probably in short supply in the years after the war. He encouraged the vestry to postpone building a hall till better conditions prevailed.

Certainly the post-war restrictions coloured the rebuilding: in March 1948 it was agreed that the floor of the chancel was to be concrete, supported by stanchions. The internal design of the chancel roof was simplified, though the vestry would not give up the rose window, and available materials were to be reused wherever possible, and even in 1950 the builder was 'making what use he could of the tinted granite in stock'. The proposed enlargement of the south wing was to be at the expense of vestry.

Despite difficulties supporting the arch during rebuilding (it was boarded off to allow services to continue in the nave), the settlement of the new foundations, and anxiety about the successful binding of the new wall to the arch, a new formal foundation stone for the chancel was laid on 7th. October, 1950.

The laying of the new foundation stone by E.E. Jewers, lay representative (extreme right) and its blessing by the Bishop. Canon Milne looks on.

After that key moment, work seems to have proceeded more successfully. A wood licence was obtained to buy timber for the chancel roof in April 1951, and the following month the eminent historian of church architecture, F.C. Eeles, visited and approved the restoration. The aumbry door, salvaged after the bombing, could be reused, and a local firm, J. & A. Ogilvie, designed the new sedilia (it cost £282.11.6 plus £15 for cushions) and repaired the communion rail. The Altar in use was suitable for installation as the High Altar. The rose window, however, continued to be the subject of dispute. The vestry hoped that Misses Chilton and Kemp of Edinburgh might design the stained glass, but it was discovered that the W.D.C. only paid out £8 per square foot for glazing and the window space was an amazing 63 square feet. When the vestry asked for temporary glass to be used until the stained glass could be purchased, the W.D.C. said they would deduct the cost of temporary glass from any future payment for stained glass. Nevertheless the plain glass had to be installed, and was never replaced.

RESTORATION OF ABERDEEN CHURCH HELD UP

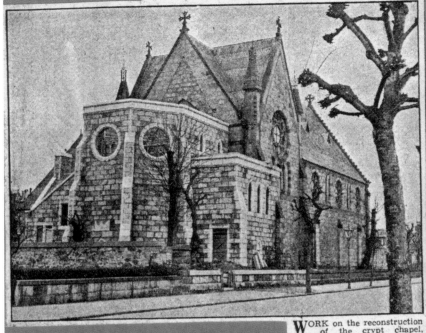

WORK on the reconstruction of the crypt chapel, chancel, sacristy and organ chamber of St Mary's Episcopal Church, Aberdeen, which were destroyed by a German bomb in April, 1943, is at present at a standstill while negotiations are in progress with the War Damage Commission.

The outer shell has been completed, with the exception of the roof of the chancel. The interior work has not yet been started.

The rector, the Rev. William Milne, told a reporter of "The Press and Journal," however, that he expects the difficulties to be cleared up in a few weeks.

He expressed the hope that the rebuilding would be completed this year.

Similar to Original

In the reconstruction of the damaged wing the builders have adopted a design similar to the original, as seen in the picture taken yesterday by a staff photographer of "The Press and Journal."

The wing will be without the very fine stained-glass windows, however, which were blown to smithereens when the bomb exploded.

Luckily, the church organ was only partly damaged at the time of the incident and is now stored in the church. Next year, it will be rebuilt at a cost of £2800 before being reinstalled.

The crypt floor was covered in Semtex – not the plastic explosive but a non-slip plastic floor paint also used on warships and described as 'seasick green', made in Barrhead. Despite the fact that the nave roof was now leaking because of the original damage from the bomb, the crypt was reconsecrated on 9th. December 1951, and the chancel was rededicated on 21st. March, 1952. A Mrs. Davie did a painted panelled frame for behind the altar, and a new reredos was made to a design by Mrs. Gellatly.

The restoration of the church was complete at last, but no vestry can rest on its laurels, and the roof was damaged again in the ferocious storm of 31st. January, 1953, when many of the woods in Aberdeenshire were flattened like skittles. However, the main attention of the vestry was now directed at the possibility of a new church hall, for use by the congregation and as an income earner for the church.

The Hall

In 1955, the 1947 plans for a new church hall were brought out again, but were found still to be too expensive to carry out. To extend the old hall was estimated to cost around £7,500, and some thought it would be worth buying the next door property, 6, Carden Terrace, and building in the garden. A few months later this was deemed unsuitable for unspecified reasons, but in February 1957 the diocese announced that St. Mark's, a mission chapel in Short Loanings, Rosemount, was to close. It had been founded in 1908 to serve the inhabitants of the surrounding tenements and factories. The building was a large iron hut, and St. Mary's vestry immediately considered it as a possible hall.

There was some excitement over this, but the building, painted grey and with green windows and doors, seems to have been in a bad state – only two hassocks were useable and worth taking to St. Mary's, and much work needed to be done, new flooring, changes to the kitchen and lavatories, and the installation of electricity. A loan was granted by the Diocese. The hall measured 990 square feet, which, it was reckoned, could accommodate 98 dancers, or 96 seated for whist, or 164 seated for concerts. The vestry acquired a licence to cover sixty occasions per year. There was a minor hall as well as the main one, but that was to be changed to make a bigger kitchen. The area was likely to be affected by local development plans but not, the Council assured the vestry, for twenty to twenty-five years. It was hoped that the restoration would pay for itself as the hall would be let to suitable parties at 5/- an hour, though soon that price went up: charities could use it for 7/6 an hour and other parties for 10/-, with an extra 2/6 for the use of the kitchen.

The site of St. Mark's Church, where once Magdala Place was laid out. The building cut across the end of the present Eden Place.

A sign of the times

The hall's window facing Magdala Place was often broken. Around 1960 glaziers came to fix it yet again and the vestry asked them to fix wires across the glass to protect it, but they said they could not: union rules forbade glaziers to work with wire.

Rectories

It is not always easy to find out where the earliest rectors of St. Mary's lived. In the census of 1861, and the valuation roll of 1862 – 1863, Rev. F.G. Lee was the tenant of Fountain Hall, after which Fountainhall Road was named, at a rent of £40 from Alexander Anderson of Rubislaw, the same man who sold Lee the land for the church building. There were two other tenants on the property: a William Smith was paying £50.4.0 in rent and James Pratt, a gardener, was paying £10.10 and £65, part of that probably for gardens. The house was large, and at that time the nearest neighbours were at Beechgrove, Mile-end House, and Whitehall, all still familiar names. On the 1868 map, it would be a pleasant country walk from there to St. Mary's: Albert Terrace was built, but Carden Place was less than half-built, with only four houses between St. Mary's and the site of the later Queen's Cross church.

In September 1866, Rev. H.J. Palmer was living in Stoneyton House, a property in the middle of Carden Place with a rateable value around half of those of its neighbours. It was also owned by Sir Alexander Anderson. Around that time a letter from Bishop Suther claims that the congregation intended to erect 'a Parsonage and Schools ... and the Trustees can secure ground contiguous to the Church for this purpose', though where this ground was is not clear.

At the beginning of 1871 Rev. H.D. Jones, who was twenty-eight and unmarried, was living as a lodger at 29, Albert Terrace, but by March 1872 he and his wife Emily were living at 6, Carden Place. Whether he moved again or not, in the same year the vestry decided to turn down an opportunity to purchase Jones' house as a rectory for £900.

Rev. J.M. Danson was living at 7, Waverly Place, in 1877 when the vestry again raised the possibility of looking for a house to buy as a parsonage. After some searching, in January 1878 12, Westfield Terrace was approved for purchase at £1,100. It had been occupied by a clothier, but in the same row were the Rev. James Selkirk of Free East Church, Rev. John Forbes, Professor of Oriental Languages, and John Christie, D.D., Professor of Church History, at Aberdeen University. Next door was Henry Alexander, editor of the *Free Press*. Danson's salary was immediately reduced to £200p.a. as he received the parsonage rent free: he had been paying around £42p.a. at Waverly Place.

7, Westfield Terrace – the street was renumbered in 1915 and this is the original No.12.

In June, 1878, a new hot water circulation system was installed, but after that there was little talk of maintaining the parsonage. The Council Sanitary Inspector inspected the house in October 1885, and condemned the building altogether as being in an unsanitary condition. None of the plumbing seemed to have suitable outlets, or to be connected with anything else. Sewage was seeping under the kitchen floor. Rev. A.S. Hill resigned, though that might have had more to do with the continued debt than with the fragrant parsonage. As usual the vestry moved with lightning speed to deal with the problem. In April 1886 they obtained an estimate from a plumber, who said 'In order to … put the Parsonage into a perfectly Sanitary State it will be necessary to go to much expense' – his estimate was £45, a considerable sum in 1886. The vestry must have decided that the expense was necessary, for in June that year the building was finally certified by the Sanitary Inspector.

The parsonage generated a little money in 1907, when Whitehall Place was extended through the back garden, but the vestry still wanted the clergy a little closer to the church. Some ground at 6, Carden Terrace, came up for sale in 1913, and it was considered for a site for a new parsonage. However, nothing happened and in 1942 Westfield Place was being decorated for the new rector – and the blackout was checked, a sign of the times.

The plumbing had never been entirely satisfactory: in 1947 it was noted that the overflow pipe from the bathroom ran out over the front door! When the church had been restored after the bombing, the search began again for a new rectory. 49, Waverley Place, was viewed, the chief advantage being the lack of a basement, the feature which had caused problems in Westfield Terrace. It sold for more than the vestry could afford. Instead, 20, Desswood Place was purchased – there was no room for a garage and the vestry had no notion of the rector having a car, so it was cheaper, and Miss Philip, a wealthy member of the congregation, lent £700 towards the purchase price of £2,500. The old rectory sold for £2,600, and Desswood Place was occupied from July 1954.

The minutes are missing for the following period, during which the property used as the Rectory changed several times. Around 1963, Desswood Place was sold and a much closer property bought, at 17, Carden Place. Canon Milne lived there for the remainder of his incumbency, as did the Rev. Thomas Turner for all of his. Rev. William McLaren, replacing Turner in 1968, may not have found it to his liking, for the next year a new rectory was found at 51, Carden Place. Again, he remained there until his resignation in 1973, when Rev. Roy Chittenden moved in. After his resignation in 1975, the vestry purchased the current Rectory, 28, Stanley Street, in January, 1976. This allowed some space for the incumbent from the church, while still placing him within easy walking distance: however, there is still no garage!

Chapter Three

The Decorations

St. Mary's with its polychromatic architecture was intended to be highly decorated in the High Church, Gothic Revival fashion, with paintings, carvings and candles everywhere.

Briefly, that *was* how it looked: this photograph shows the chancel decorated for Christmas around 1865. Here we can see how bright the decorated ceiling was in its original form. A letter from F.G. Lee to Francis Christie in 1889 shows how bitterly he felt the opposition to his decoration, even a quarter of a century later:

The high altar was robbed of its tabernacle, and painted all over with [illegible] gimcracks; the rood and figures were removed, and everything altered down to the vulgarest and most commonplace level. The crypt, too, was turned into a coal-cellar, I was told.

Paintings

Lee had already written to Christie in 1887: 'The picture of the Crucifixion after a rough suggestion of my own was drawn by Mr. N.J.H. Westlake: as was also that of the B.V. Mary (a personal gift to myself) which was over a side altar in the nave to the north of the choir.' Nathaniel Hubert John Westlake was a Gothic Revival artist working with the firm Lavers & Barraud, Ecclesiastical Designers, from the 1850s. The firm also designed the stained glass windows in the chancel.

Christie had apparently written to ask if the triptych was by the famous Aberdeen artist and churchman, William Dyce, who had been a great influence on Westlake. Lee, however, affirmed that there was nothing by Dyce in the church. He did, however, claim that Dyce's picture in black chalk on brown paper of Bishop Matthew Parker had been painted at Lee's suggestion and was much published after Dyce's death.

Westlake's triptych was repaired in May 1903, as the colours were coming away: the wall behind it was probably damp. It was suggested by the vestry that Phoebe Traquair might do the repair, but in the end it was fixed by Hay & Lyall in Aberdeen. In 1929 a new reredos was presented by Alexander and Ann Cheyne in memory of Agnes Cheyne[2], and the Westlake triptych was removed to the crypt.

The Cheyne reredos was made by Faith Craft Studios, London, and the artist was W. Lawson.

On 1st. March, 1943, the reredos was removed from the sacristy to the church, so that Mr. Jackson Simpson of Aberdeen Art Gallery could pronounce on its artistic merit. It was therefore

---

[2] This was probably the Agnes Cheyne in Annfield Terrace who died aged 77 in 1927, leaving a husband, printer Alexander Cheyne, and a daughter Ann.

presumably saved when the church was bombed the following month. Whatever the verdict was, it is clear from the photograph of the rededication service in 1952 that the Westlake reredos had been restored to the chancel, and the whereabouts of the Cheyne reredos are currently unknown.

In the early twentieth century a new altarpiece was installed in the crypt, painted by Arthur E. Payne of the Aberdeen School of Art. 'The picture represents, in the Centre, the Blessed Virgin and the Divine Child, surrounded by rays; and beneath six Saints viz St. Andrew, St. Columba, St. Machar, St. Margaret of Scotland, St. Drostane and St. Francis of Assissi'[3]. This was presumably destroyed in the bombing, and only one rather poor photograph is left as evidence.

There is no evidence that Lee had been correctly informed that the crypt was used as a coal cellar: the rood beam, too, was never as bare as he had been led to believe. Rev. A. Rudall had painted

---

[3] Vestry minutes.

'God forbid that I should glory save in the Cross of Our Lord Jesus Christ' on the bare rood beam, and this was occasionally covered over with appropriate paper quotations depending on the season, presumably by death-defying vestry members on long ladders. In 1927, the Mothers' Guild asked the vestry to have erected on the rood beam the symbolised figures of Calvary as a memorial to the late Sister Amy of the House of Bethany. Mr. Townend of the Art Gallery was consulted and presumably approved, and the figures that Bishop Suther had forbidden were replaced.

In December, 1907, the vestry was told that

> Mr. Allan Sutherland, artist, had offered to decorate the panels in the nave of the church with a series of paintings.

The fresco of the Annunciation in the north-west corner of the church was therefore painted by Aberdeen-born artist Allan N. Sutherland (1883 – 1918) in 1908, at a cost of £9.4.6 for materials. It seems in places not quite finished: Mary's left hand and Gabriel's face in particular seem to have been left incomplete. There is no record that he started any of the other panels, and Sutherland died in the First World War. In the 1970s, according to anecdotes, the middle panel on the south side was painted with a picture of a deer, but after that all the currently blank panels were painted blue, then white.

The tondo above the Green Organ to the south of the chancel is a copy of Raphael's *Madonna of the Pomegranate*, bought by members of the congregation from a Mrs. Davie in 1956, for £45. The circular aperture was originally for organ pipes when the organ was situated on the north side of the chancel, and other covers have occasionally filled the space.

In the porch, the painting above the doorway comes from Cyprus and was brought back by a member of the congregation to be installed by Margaret Johnston who commissioned it in memory of her mother, Susan Murdoch. Sadly, Mrs. Johnston died before it was installed and it was therefore decided that it should commemorate her, too.

Carvings and furnishings

Lightfoot's short history gives us evidence of some of the

furnishings destroyed in the bombing:

> The magnificent stone mensa or Altar-slab of polished red granite was the gift of G.J.R. Gordon of Ellon and was supported on four short pillars of granite with carved stone capitals.

This has of course been replaced with the present grey granite table, considerably smaller than the original. It is similar to the old crypt table, with a plainer incised Celtic cross in the centre.

In 1886 Christie asked for a pulpit to be installed in the church for the first time, and Arthur Clyne was asked to design it.

> Aberdeen had enjoyed the extraordinary ecclesiastical pyrotechnics of John Bridgeford Pirie (1852 – 1890) and his partner Arthur Clyne (1852 – 1923).
>
> *Scottish Architects' Papers*

Clyne had strong Episcopalian connexions, and was the joint founder of Aberdeen Ecclesiological Society. He designed St. Margaret's, Braemar, and St. Devenick's, Bieldside, but also worked on Queen's Cross Church, and St. Andrew's Cathedral (the reredos is his), St. John's, St. James', and St. Mark's. The pulpit was first used on 17th. November, 1886, and £26.13.2 was paid to the carpenter. Christie introduced some further furnishings and remarked in the church magazine:

> The Hymn Board has arrived – and a very nice one it is ...

It is often hard to trace where specific furnishings came from, as many gifts were anonymous. In 1908 an anonymous donor presented the carved wooden eagle lectern we use today, and the old brass lectern was given to St. Mark's Mission in Short Loanings. The Austrian oak clergy and choir stalls were also given by an anonymous donor in 1913. The two deep carvings on the clergy stalls depict Our Lord and St. Thomas, and Job and his friends: the designs were by William Kelly, and were carried out by William Banburh, RBS, of Gray's School of Art. William Kelly also designed the altar rail, installed in memory of Canon Christie in 1924. Originally with a space of five feet between the two rails, the space was reduced when the rail was repaired and reinstalled after the bombing.

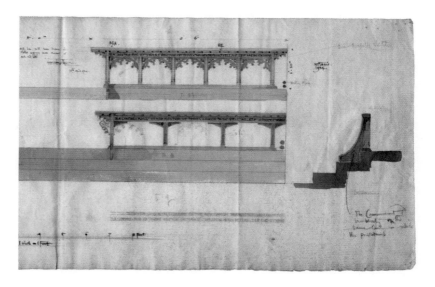

Part of William Kelly's two possible designs for the altar rail[4]

The old seats were given to St. Clement's, at that time down by Footdee. In the early years of the twentieth century there was a men's carving guild active in the church, and several pieces of furniture seem to have been made by its members, again anonymously.

One piece of furniture, however, has a very distinct origin and provenance. Arthur Gascoigne Douglas, son of the Earl of Morton, was rector of Shapwick parish in Dorset from 1872 to 1883, and renovated the church while he was there. In particular he removed and replaced a little altar and a prie-dieu, and took these with him when he was appointed Bishop of Aberdeen in 1883. He used them to furnish his private chapel at Bishop's Court in Albyn Place. In 1943, Bishop Hall was to move from Bishop's Court to a smaller residence, and as St. Mary's was in dire need of furnishings after the bombing, the altar and prie-dieu were presented. The altar dates from 1650 and is solid oak. The triptych above it is in the style of William Dyce but is unattributed.

---

[4] William Kelly's design: Aberdeen University Library MS3759/A1/15, part.

Embroideries[5]

Amongst the items listed as furnishings of St. John's Church, Crown Terrace, in the time of Rev. Patrick Cheyne, were two banners, simply designed, one showing the cross of St. Andrew and the other that of St. George. There are no later inventories of St. John's, but in the *Church Times* article on St. Mary's temporary chapel in 1863, it mentions amongst the High Church procession

... banners with crosses of St. Andrew and St. George.

Coincidence? The banners appear again in the 1865 photograph at the beginning of this chapter. However, the current banners are modern ones: the St. Andrew's Cross was made for the 140th anniversary of St. Mary's in 2003, and the Magnificat banner the following year, both by a group of members of the congregation.

Older embroideries do survive in the church. The communion table cloth or altar frontal seen in the photograph of the Cheyne reredos above, depicting the Annunciation, is in three frames at the back of the church, conserved by Prue King of the congregation and framed by Dennis Leiper of the Riverside Gallery in Stonehaven at a cost of £210 in 1997. The silk was disintegrating badly and coming away in flakes, so the panel was divided into three and mounted on to washed cotton on conservation board. There is no evidence as to the source of this frontal, though it might be a patronal frontal worked by one of the great London houses at the time the church was established. It is reminiscent of the work of G.F. Watts, but the Watts studio lost most of their documents during the war. David Gazeley of Watts and Co. in Tufton Street, Westminster (the recognised authority on church textiles of the period), has commented:

The overall style and colouring would suggest the high Victorian period, 1850 – 1870. All the designs are well-drawn and vigorous. The artist had a good grasp of the stylistic vocabulary which they were using. The background silk damask was manufactured

---

[5] My thanks to Prue King for her expert notes and investigations on church embroideries.

by Warners and dates from the period. The gold orphrey braid used on each side of the 'lily' panel was designed by A.W.N. Pugin and distributed through Hardman's of Birmingham. I do not believe that this frontal has anything to do with either of these two people. I particularly like the veining in the marble columns which support the canopy over the figures of the angel and Our Lady, this is an unusual idea. My overall impression is that the frontal was originally very nice and professionally worked, with a strong sense of working within a very particular and distinct style, which may or may not be the architectural style of the church building.

Another communion table cloth is framed and in use as a reredos in the chapel at the back of the church, depicting Christ in Majesty.

The central panel of the altar frontal. The photograph also includes some of the painted decoration of the nave, indicating the kind of setting for which the frontal was intended.

David Gazeley again remarks:

> I would consider this a work of considerable art. I
> would suggest that it was made at about the same
> time as the Annunciation Frontal, but it is in every
> way far superior as a work of art. It appears that the
> central figure of Christ in Majesty has been renewed
> at some point incorporating the original head and
> crown, and possibly the roses on the throne. Special
> note should be taken of the embroidered border on
> each side of the figures of St. Peter and St. Paul.
> These are of exceptional design quality and remind
> me of the work of Owen Jones and Christopher
> Dresser, two great Victorian pattern designers. I have
> rarely seen such a well drawn vigorous and truly
> artistic frontal of its date before.

Again, it is unknown where this was made: St. Margaret's
Episcopal Convent on the Spital, Aberdeen, was well known for its
fine embroidery, but there is no mention of this piece in its
admittedly incomplete archive.

The Rector's Wife is Overruled

Mrs. Milne objected to the purchase of a poppy wreath on the
grounds that it was not in keeping with the decorations in the church.

Sundries

Though there was tension over the church's decorations in
the first few years of its history, Canon Christie was the first
incumbent to be forthright about them in the church magazine, and
he did not confine himself to compliments.

Christmas Decorations – We again record our gratitude to our helpers within and without our own circle. Their work is very tasteful, and does not err in being overdone; but a few shrubs in pots would have enhanced the effect very much.

January 1887

A new Font Ewer, of lacquered brass, has been got from Messrs. Pratt & Sons, London, to replace the unseemly tin can hitherto used.

1890

There were many changes and renewals in Christie's time, again some of them anonymous in origin. A brass altar cross arrived via Cox & Sons, London, anonymously, at Christmas 1890. In March 1897 'the rector was authorised to dispose of the Brass Corona, the two standards and the picture of the Old Pelican in any way he wished' (vestry minutes). In 1891 gas pendants were designed for the church by Arthur Clyne, in the form of six pendant coronas and one small standard light near pulpit, and he then designed a lantern for the porch in 1904. The lighting in the church was electrified in 1911. A Sanctuary lamp donated by Mrs. W. Anderson of Queen's Road in memory of her mother was made by Faith Craft Studios who designed the Cheyne reredos, but after the bombing it was replaced by one from Mrs. Crichton in memory of her husband, the Rev. W.I. Crichton, who had been Diocesan Chaplain from 1938 to 1945 and had died in 1947. Former incumbents were remembered: E. Lightfoot donated two oak candlesticks (currently at the altar at the back of the church) for the chancel in memory of his father, and the congregation raised money for a chalice and patten, based on a 16th. century pattern. This work was carried out after the bombing: the original chalice was damaged but was completely repaired for £33.

An 1899 inventory mentions an antique brass alms basin from Venice and twenty alms bags, five in each of the liturgical colours, green, purple, red and white or gold, except for black. The 1964 inventory lists a harmonium, two processional crosses, two alms plates, thirty-six alms bags and one alms basin, but the censers and incense boats mentioned in the 1899 inventory have vanished. The furnishings in 1964 were insured for £2,850, the organ for £3,500, the rectory for £4,850, and the church building for £30,000: these sums would not go far to replacing any of these things today!

Chapter Four

The Music

     The first mention of music in connexion with St. Mary's is in the new church at the licensing service, where at both morning and evening service the music of Thomas Tallis and Thomas Helmore was used and the anthem on both occasions was from King Solomon's prayer at the dedication of the Temple, viz. 'O Lord, my

God, hear Thou the prayer thy servant prayeth." by S.S. Wesley. The organist was John Fraser, a member of the congregation whose father was also part of the church, and the organ, by Bevington and Sons, London[6], as Lee remembered years later, came from a church in Kent: the organ loft was specially built to accommodate it in the south chancel, in the space now occupied by the sacristy. The pipes spoke through a large round opening in the wall where there is now a picture, above where the Samuel Green chamber organ is now situated.

John Fraser survived as organist only for four years. In May 1869, he was forced to remit his office and keys for failing to turn up at a service with no warning, and presumably no good excuse. He was the first in a line of church organists of whom we know very little, despite their playing a significant part in the quality and style of worship at St. Mary's.

Fraser's replacement was S. Dennett, 175 George Street, appointed in November 1869. Less than a month later the Bishop, still rather sensitive about St. Mary's, demanded that Dennett be dismissed for being 'insolent' to the Bishop. The vestry considered the matter and quietly let it fade away, perhaps considering that Bishops were more easily replaced than church organists (plus ça change!). He was paid £20p.a., and maybe this was not enough, for Dennett faded from the record in 1877 and after enquiries as far afield as England, John Kirby was appointed organist at £30p.a. in September 1877.

Kirby was replaced by Septimus Parker, a music teacher, who died of bronchitis in 1886. By then Francis Christie was rector and his arguments for raising the organist's salary appeared in the church announcements with typical Christie verve:

> without this [£50p.a.] we will not be able to get and
> KEEP a good Organist and Choir Trainer.

With this substantial rise in pay, at a time when the church was still in debt, the vestry appointed a Mr. Brumten, who had been organist in the Earl of Aberdeen's new interdenominational chapel at Haddo. Despite the pay, he resigned in January 1890, and was

---

[6] David A. Stewart: *Organs in Scotland: An Interim List*, Edinburgh Society of Organists, 1985

replaced by Sydney Townshend in April of that year. Townshend, of 28, St Swithin Street, started with some energy, founding a music class for boys that brought more families into the congregation. He and Canon Christie between them took a keen interest not only in the musical talents of the choirboys but also in their prospects in the world: one member of the congregation now remembers how her father was advised to enter the bank, which resulted in a successful career, lifelong associations with China and Singapore, and four generations attending St. Mary's. Townshend brought his own family into the congregation, too: his daughter Hilda was baptised at St. Mary's in August the same year.

In that month, the vestry set up a system of payment for choristers, £5 for the men and various levels of payment for the boys. Despite this enthusiasm, Townshend left for St. Machar's Cathedral in December 1891 (where he only stayed for two years and where his name appears as 'Townsend'), and Mr. David Lawrie was appointed.

In 1895, thirty years after the church was built, there was a general campaign for a new organ. It was bought from Abbott & Smith, Blackman Lane, Leeds, for £400. The firm had been in business since 1869 (and were to exhibit at major venues, including the Scottish National Exhibition in Edinburgh), but the partners were experienced organ builders before joining forces. Abbott & Smith suggested two additional stops, the open diapason in the pedal and the salicional in the great organ omitting the Bass Flute, for an extra £60, and the vestry agreed. That Abbott & Smith suggested additional stops indicates that perhaps the organ was not new, but a rebuild from another church.

The organ was inaugurated with a recital by Dr. A.L. Peace, a gifted English organist and composer who was at that time organist at Glasgow Cathedral. Another stop was added to the organ by E.H. Lawton, a local tuner and organ-builder, in 1899, starting a relationship between organ and tuner which continued until Lawton's death in the 1940s.

Lawrie, a music seller in Victoria Street, died of tuberculosis in February 1902, aged only thirty-three. A new organist, Cyril Harrison from Tain, was appointed, and had new powers to fine choirboys for misbehaviour. New choir pews were designed by architect Arthur Clyne (the old ones were donated to St. Margaret's

Church, Gallowgate), but Harrison left in September 1905.

Description of the Abbott & Smith Organ, 1895:

	Great Organ	Ft.	Pipes		Swell Organ	Ft.	Pipes
1	Large Open Diapason	8	58	1	Lieblich Bourdon	16	58
2	Salicional	8	58	2	Open Diapason	8	58
3	Hohl Flote	8	58	3	Lieblich Gedact	8	58
4	Vox Angelica	8	58	4	Violin-e-Cello	8	58
5	Principal	4	58	5	Voix Celestes	8	49
6	Harmonic Flute	4	58	6	Gemshorn	4	58
7	Flautina	2	58	7	Horn	8	58
8	Clarinet	8	58	8	Oboe	8	58
	Total Pipes	464			Total Pipes	455	

	Pedal Organ				Couplers
1	Open Diapason	16	30	1	Swell Super Octave
2	Bourdon	16	30	2	Swell to Great
	Total Pipes		60	3	Swell to Pedal
				4	Great to Pedal

Composition Pedals
3 acting on Great and Pedal Organs
2 acting on Swell Organ

Another new organist, Andrew C. Kidd of 48, St. Swithin Street, was appointed at the salary of £40 - 45p.a. (less than the sum recommended by Canon Christie twenty years earlier!). He too was a music seller with one brother a music teacher: five grown-up children all lived at home with their mother. E.H. Lawton installed a water motor for the organ which had previously been hand-pumped: the work was scheduled to be done at the same time as similar work at North Parish Church, as it required the opening and closing of streets for laying new lead pipes. In 1906, the organ was valued for insurance at £500.

For additional music in the church and the new choir vestry, a piano by Payne of London was bought for £27 in 1914. Kidd however was made to resign as organist, as he persisted in turning up late for services. Miss Ella M. McLeod, the first female organist, was appointed, but left again in 1916 despite being much liked. She was replaced by Mr. George Henry of 14, Wallfield Place.

In 1916, Lawton renovated the 1896 Abbott and Smith. Apart from a cleaning and some revoicing of the reeds, he added a new tremulant and electrified the blowing system.

This photograph shows the Choir and Canon Christie in the 1920s, as identified by a member of the congregation whose mother was a choir member. Women first joined the choir in the 1920s but were not robed until 1932, as in the photograph below.

The Choir at the church, 1930s

There was a shortage of boys for the choir at the time, but more were sought. Mr. Henry, one of the longest serving organists in the church's history, died in October 1932. He was only forty-four, and died of a combination of influenza, emphysema, septic pneumonia and cardiac failure: it is interesting to note that several organists died quite young in post of chest-related illnesses. A Mr. Sefton was appointed, and several choir boys immediately left! It is not recorded whether or not they returned when Sefton resigned only four years later to take up the post of housemaster at the Episcopal Church-linked Aberlour Children's Home. E. Stonebanks took over in November 1936, but left to join the RAF in December 1940 and Jenkyn Jones was appointed interim organist.

The Second World War of course had a severe effect on St. Mary's, though as late as 1942 the choir were still active in Midnight Eucharist on Christmas Eve – the male choir members had the important and difficult task of attending to the blackout. However, the organ was very badly damaged in the bombing of April 1943, and by October of that year, with the surviving parts of the organ laid up in Lawton's yard and no chancel to put them in, the Rector was looking for a second-hand Hammond organ for the church. In June 1945, when Jones had left and Stonebanks had not returned from the war, Mr. George Trash, organist at St Andrew's cathedral, offered to help find a replacement organ by advertising for one as a gift or loan. Second-hand organs were very difficult to come by, but the Board of Trade, who ran the War Damage Commission, agreed to pay for the continued storage of the organ parts at Lawton's. Then a fire at Lawton's premises in Ardarroch Road caused further damage. Stonebank, who had never officially returned to his duties, gave in his resignation and Mr. A.N. Pugh of 61, Angusfield Avenue, was appointed. The search for a replacement organ continued and in March 1946 the vestry advertised for a small organ in the *Church Times*, *The Times*, *The Scotsman* and *The Daily Telegraph*. There was still no response, and at last in May Lawton came to the rescue: Miss Leith of the Isle of Wight, formerly of Oyne, had a pipe organ in storage at Lawton's and wanted it to go to a museum or church, and Lawton suggested St. Mary's. Both parties were delighted, and a plate was designed to fix to the organ. It was carefully insured for £250, and the Green Organ arrived at St. Mary's. This removal of the

Green organ to St. Mary's and its setting up was Lawton's last completed work.

Now established to the south side of the chancel, the Green Organ was built by Samuel Green (1740 – 1796). His organs are also in Kensington Palace (moved from Buckingham Palace in 2002), in Canterbury Cathedral, and in the Royal Naval College Chapel, Greenwich.

This organ was built in 1778: it is of national historic importance and holds a Grade 1 listed Certificate from the British Institute of Organ Studies. The case is believed to be by Chippendale, and the organ has been visited by several organ historians, as well as by Ralph Vaughan Williams and Herbert Howells: the latter wrote two pieces of music for it, Dalby's Fancy and Dalby's Toccata (1959). (which were played by the late Donald Hawksworth for the Scottish Federation of Organists at its 2009 annual conference here in St Mary's, Carden Place, Aberdeen). The organ was built for Sir William Gordon of Oyne, Aberdeenshire, and gifted to St. Mary's by his great-granddaughter Mary Leith in 1946 after the destruction of the main church organ in 1943. The Aberdeen-born composer Martin

Dalby (son of the dedicatee above) has also written music especially for this instrument: Martin Dalby's Fantasia (1964) was dedicated to Donald Hawksworth.

The specification is:

Open Diapason	8	Stopped Diapason Treble	8
Stopped Diapason Bass	8	Principal Treble	4
Principal Bass	4	Fifteenth Treble	2
Fifteenth Bass	2	Swelling Hautboy	8

Pedal operating "nag's head" swell for Hautboy
Pedal removing Principal and Fifteenth

A connexion with a sister church

Norman and Beard (before Hill joined them) were founded in Diss, Norfolk, whose principal church St Mary the Virgin, Diss, has close links with us here at St Mary's, Carden Place.

A year later, in 1947, another crisis occurred: E.H. Lawton died, the business was closed, and the property was to be sold. Roberts (Aberdeen) Ltd. bought the site but were using Lawton's old yard for storage, so were happy to go on storing the main organ. The vestry were not so happy, however, and the parts of the organ were moved back to the church and stored at the west end. This seems to have stimulated the repair process and at last the organ was reinstalled and rededicated on 16th. October, 1952. This rebuild was carried out by the renowned firm of Hill, Norman and Beard (this firm had been looking after the organ in St Andrew's Cathedral when George Trash was the organist there, and he was also organ consultant for St Mary's at this time). At this point the organ chamber was moved from the south chancel to its present position in the north chancel, the console remaining at the south side, with electric action to the new chamber. All this effort had to be appreciated, and in February 1953 the vestry remarked that the organist, Pugh, was not making the most of the newly rebuilt organ in terms of variety, and Pugh resigned forthwith. Brian Simpson, who had been the organist at St. Paul's, Aberdeen, was appointed in April at £80p.a. His salary was increased to £100p.a. in October 1956.

The choir with Canon Milne, early 1950s: the picture includes Catherine Booth, later Taylor (second from right) and Brenda Lyon, later Lees (third from right). Catherine Booth was the daughter of the Rector's warden, Bob Booth, and married the head server, F. Taylor. Their daughter Gillian (now Gillian Jack) who grew up at St. Mary's later had a career with Scottish Opera, then with English National Opera.

Brian Simpson, born in 1927, was involved in the music of the Diocese for all of his life. He joined the Cathedral choir as a young boy in 1936 and eventually became senior chorister. In the 1950s and 1960s when he was organist and choirmaster at St. Mary's, the choir was around forty strong, and he earned much praise for his ability to direct and guide singers of all ages. Outside the church, he was a mathematician and had a fine reputation as a teacher. Before retirement he was Depute Head at Westhill Academy. While it is interesting to note that St. Mary's has mostly engaged professional musicians as organists, Brian Simpson was an exception. Following disagreements he resigned twice, yet he undoubtedly left his mark on the musical life of the congregation.

St. Mary's Choir lead the singing of Christmas carols at Aberdeen Joint Railway Station, 1963

Many people feel a special atmosphere when they enter St. Mary's, and music, the organs and fine acoustics have inspired many celebrated events over the years. As well as his organ music already mentioned, the eminent Scottish composer Martin Dalby, one time school-boy chorister at St. Mary's who went on to become head of music at BBC Scotland, wrote a Benedictus and Jubilate for St. Mary's in 1963. Some time later the BBC also broadcast some programmes from St. Mary's featuring the Samuel Green organ, with Martin Dalby's father, John, as organist. Tapes still exist, as they do of the broadcast of a Sunday service in July 1981, where the Abbot and Smith / Hill, Norman and Beard organ can clearly be heard. The rector then was Canon Jim Alexander, whose daughter Helen was the BBC producer in charge of the broadcast. St. Mary's has also played host, most recently in 2009, to the Annual Conference of the Scottish Federation of Organists.

The Main Organ

The current main church organ was originally built in 1876 by Forster and Andrews, a very reputable firm, for Blackfriars Congregational Church. In 1886 it was moved, along with the congregation(!) to the new Congregational Church in Skene Street. It was moved by Wadsworth Brothers (who by then had a branch at 38 Market Street, Aberdeen, with John Wardle as manager) and the move included some minor tonal adjustments. At Skene Street it was played by local character Verden Henderson Sykes, who named it 'Bessie'. There it remained until Skene Street Church closed in 1975, when the well-known Liverpool firm Rushworth & Dreaper transplanted it again to John Knox Church, Mounthooly, with further modifications. In 2000, as John Knox Church was to become flats, it was moved finally to St. Mary's, Carden Place, where the action was completely renewed (tracker/mechanical) and the organ rebuilt by A.F. Edmonstone of Forteviot. It was consecrated for use here in May 2000.

It has always been a 2-manual and pedal instrument. Two of the ranks of pipes of the present instrument were retained from St Mary's original Abbot and Smith/Hill Norman and Beard organ. The stop-list is modest but versatile and the pipe-work of fine quality, its tone enhanced by the sympathetic acoustics of the building.

The specification is:

Great		Swell		Pedal	
Open Diapason	8	Open Diapason	8	Open Diapason	16
Claribel Flute	8	Lieblich Gedact	8	Bourdon	16
Principal	4	Viola	8	Principal	8
Wald Flute	4	Voix Celestes	8		
Twelfth	$2\,^2/_3$	Principal		4	
Fifteenth	2	Principal		2	
Mixture	III ranks	Sesquialtera		II ranks	
Trumpet	8				

Great to Pedal, Swell to Pedal, Swell to Great, Balanced Swell Pedal

It is interesting that both Abbott & Smith, St Mary's original organ-builders, and Forster & Andrews, builders of the present organ, were both very highly regarded by the famous and outstanding German builder Edmund Schultze who did much work in Britain, and whose work influenced both these English firms, which adds a certain cohesiveness and continuity of provenance to our present organ.

The acoustics of St. Mary's lend themselves to many types of musical performance, and in recent years they have enhanced woodwind instruments, pianos, electric guitars and on several occasions steel drums, as well as the traditional choral singing and organ playing.

Various organists followed Brian Simpson, including Dr. G. Bulmer, interestingly another scientist, from RGIT. Peter Hayman then served as interregnum and was good at recruiting boys for the choir (as can be seen from the photograph below) but it was felt he lacked competency as an organist and to his chagrin he was never officially appointed. He married choir member Jean Brunton, and both went on to appear as soloists in future concerts at the church under the next organist and choirmaster, Geoffrey Atkinson (1970 – 1976), now editor and publisher of church music at Fagus Music.

St. Mary's Choir, May 1970

During his tenure, Geoffrey Atkinson continued to promote concerts with the choir, some accompanied by full orchestra. There were also occasional instrumental recitals of chamber music making use of the Samuel Green organ. The flautist in one such recital was one Ann Lennox, a seventeen-year-old schoolgirl already of striking ability and appearance – who was to become rather more famous a little later … as Annie Lennox.

More recently, in the 1990s and 2000s Northern Voices and their conductor Geoffrey Atkinson, by then (and still) organist next door at Queen's Cross Church, presented many recitals in St. Mary's, with Geoffrey sharing the conducting and organ-playing with Kyle McCallum, St. Mary's present organist. Even more recently we have been delighted to share full Choral Evensong services with Queen's Cross Church Choir under Geoffrey and Kyle, these now becoming regular annual events.

After Atkinson's move to Queen's Cross in 1976 subsequent St. Mary's organists included Claire Mingins, Michael Mappin, who went on to become a presenter on the newly-fledged Classic *fm*, Dr. David Smith, now Professor of Music at Aberdeen University, and William Henderson, now at St Andrew's Cathedral. In 2005, Kyle McCallum was appointed. He had been an organist in the Church of Scotland since the 1970s but was delighted to 'change sides' when he came to St. Mary's! He has been an instrumental tutor at the University of Aberdeen and with the Shire's Instrumental Music Service, was previously Director of Music at Rannoch School and organist of Dunkeld Cathedral, and has been president of the Scottish Federation of Organists. He has continued to promote church music and the instruments at the disposal of St. Mary's[7].

---

[7] Thanks to Kyle McCallum, the present organist, for his help and his descriptions and pictures of the main and Green organs, and other information, to Jean Hamilton for memories of her father's connexion with the choir, to Christian Hutcheon for her memories of the choir in the 1920s and 1930s, to Malcolm Hay for his photographs of the choir in the 1950s and 1960s, to Andrew Armstrong for his memories of Brian Simpson, and to Norman Marr for his memories of Verden Henderson Sykes and other information.

Chapter Five

Wartime

The First World War had remarkably little impact on church life in Aberdeen. At St. Margaret's Convent, for example, the main concerns were the deportation of a German sister, and the visits of another sister to Oldmill Hospital where her brother was receiving physiotherapy. At St. Mary's, similarly, there is mention of a vestry member, Robert Scott, who enlisted as Major in the 4th. Gordon Highlanders in November 1914, and the Aberdeen Bach Choir used the church for a Belgian Relief Fund concert in 1915. An Army Service Corps wagon being used by the Aberdeen Coastal Defence crashed into the church railings in 1917, and caused some damage. However, the congregation did lose ten men from amongst them or associated with them, of the 91 men and four women (a doctor and three nurses) who served in the conflict. The war memorial was proposed as early as 22nd. November, 1918, and designed by William Kelly, though Mr. Porter, whose son had served and been awarded the M.C., did not approve of any war memorial that did not serve some practical purpose. The names commemorated on it are as follows:

- Lance Corporal Thomas Anderson, 4th. Gordon Highlanders, son of Thomas and Mary Ann Anderson, 221, Great Northern Road. He died on 23rd. September, 1917, aged 27, and is buried in Dozingheim Military Cemetery.

- Lance Corporal James Sharp Arthur, 4th. Gordon Highlanders, brother of Mrs. M. Farquhar, 88, Leadside Road. He died on 9th. April, 1917, and is commemorated on the Arras Memorial.

- Private John Smith McKay, 8th/10th. Gordon Highlanders, son of William and Mary Ann McKay, Muchalls, Stonehaven, and wife of Henrietta Russell McKay, 12, Watson Street, Aberdeen. He died aged 28 on 23rd. August, 1917, and is commemorated on the Tyne Cot Memorial.

- Private Charles Pithie, 18th. Glasgow Yeomanry Battalion, Highland Light Infantry, son of Mrs. Charles Pithie, Craigleig Cottage, 67, Prospect Terrace, Aberdeen. He died aged 25 on 25th. March, 1918, and is commemorated on the Pozieres Memorial.

- Private Gildart Jackson Walker, VII Canadians, son of Annie Walker, 15 Dee Place, and late Rev. G. B. Walker. He died aged 36 on 15th. August, 1917, and is commemorated on the Vimy Memorial

- Private Charles Bernard Mozley, 4th. Regiment, South African Infantry (South Africa Scots), son of Catherine Primrose Mozley, late of Albyn Grove, Aberdeen, and the late Charles Mozley, FRHS, of Cambridge. He was an employee of Mackay Bros and McMahon, Durban. He died aged 26 on 17th. July, 1916, and is commemorated on the Thiepval Memorial.

- Private James Henderson, 1st. Scots Guards, son of James and Louisa Henderson, 116, Hardgate. He died aged 19 on 10th. March, 1918, and is buried at Fampoux Cemetery.

- Corporal John Charles Lewis, E Battalion, Tank Corps, son of James and Catherine Lewis, 28, Allan Street. He died aged 25 on 23rd. November, 1917, and is commemorated on the Cambrai Memorial.

- Gunner Dennis McAnulty, Royal Garrison Artillery. No records. It seems likely that he was related to James McAnulty who appears in the Book of Remembrance for 1918 when he died aged 45: his father, a pedlar, was named Dennis, and was still apparently alive in 1918. The family lived in Jack's Brae.

- Lieutenant Noel Douglas Bayly, 2 Company 2nd. Battalion, Irish Guards, only son of Annie Lilla Bayly (nee Douglas), 3 Tite Street, Chelsea, and the late Major Henry Bayly, Gordon Highlanders. He died aged 28 27/11/1917, and is buried at Anneux British Cemetery.

The War Memorial was in the church by November 1919, and a roll was prepared of all who had served. However, one war casualty was not mentioned on the war memorial, for he died in 1919.

William Griffiths Bain Minto was born at 8, Westfield Terrace, Aberdeen, on 13th. November 1880, the elder son of Professor William Minto who held the Chair of English and Logic at Aberdeen University until his early death in 1892. His mother was Cornelia Beatrice Minto, daughter of an English clergyman. He attended Aberdeen University and was president, at various times, of the Students' Representative Council, the Debating Society, the Liberal Association and the Students' Union, as well as being a keen hockey player. After graduating M.A. from Aberdeen University in 1901, William G.B. Minto became a law agent in 1906, and a partner in the Aberdeen firm of Booth, Mintos and Morrison, solicitors, where the senior partner was his stepfather, Williamson Booth. Straight after graduation, he was commissioned as second lieutenant in what was then the Aberdeen Volunteer Artillery, and when the volunteer forces became the Territorial Army he was promoted Major in the North of Scotland Royal Garrison Artillery Territorial Force. At the beginning of the First World War he was in charge of Torry Battery and later worked at Broughty Ferry before taking 151st. Seige Battery to France in 1916. He received the Territorial Decoration, and was promoted again to Garrison Commander at Aberdeen. According to his obituary in the *Aberdeen University Review*, he 'carried out the important duties of the post with the utmost efficiency and success'.

On 28th. June, 1919, at the age of 38, he was to take part in firing a salute in celebration of the signing of the peace with Germany. However, during the preparation of a naval gun at Torry Battery a blank cartridge exploded, Minto was injured, and he died of his injuries at Aberdeen Royal Infirmary four days later, on 2nd. July, 1919. Although his name does not appear on the War Memorial in St. Mary's, it is on the War Memorial in Allenvale Cemetery, where he is also buried. A separate tablet to Lt. Col. Minto was designed by William Kelly and made by Birmingham Art Guild. It was dedicated by the Bishop in December 1920 in the presence of the officers, NCOs and men of the North of Scotland Royal Garrison Artillery.

The Second World War was initially much more trouble to the congregation at St. Mary's. In January 1940 the vestry noted that it was difficult holding meetings at night because of the blackout, and for Midnight Eucharist on Christmas Eve, 1942, the male members of the choir had the tricky job of arranging the blackout of the church. The organist, Stonebanks, left to join the RAF in December 1940, and the treasurer, William Sutherland, enlisted in the army in November 1942, though his accountancy firm would continue making up the accounts. The cost of air raid protection had to be met, and the vestry decided to allocate money to it from the Fabric Fund.

It was difficult to preserve the aesthetics of the church in wartime, and the railings were removed for the war effort, though when the fire service asked if they could place a water tank in front of the church in January 1942, Canon Lightfoot insisted it be placed behind instead.

The vestry also had to insure against enemy action: Aberdeen had been hit a few times already by October 1941 when the church furniture was insured at £1,500 and the organ also at £1,500 for six months. In March 1943, the vestry was asked whether or not the church building itself was insured against war damage, and the vestry reported back on 1st. April:

At the end of the war Churches will be restored free of charge – by the Government – to the owners, but only after consultation with the Ecclesiastical Authorities concerned and their deciding that it is in the interests of the church as a whole that the church destroyed should be rebuilt.

The timing of this enquiry was, as it turned out, significant, for on the night of 21st. April, 1943, on the worst night of Aberdeen's blitz, the church was hit by a 500kg. thin walled cluster bomb, which went straight through the chancel into the crypt and exploded. That night the buildings hit included Causewayend Church in Powis Place; Gordon's College, Schoolhill; Hutcheon Street Meat Mart; Richards, Ltd. and the electrical substation in Maberly Street; Kittybrewster Station; the Royal Infirmary; Cornhill Hospital; NORCO at Berryden; St. Peter's cemetery; Middlefield School; and the Don Paper Mill. On the same night, the entire Porter family, members of the congregation, were killed when a bomb hit their tenement flat in Bedford Road.

Recently, the Kings, members of the congregation, recalled the day after the bombing:

John remembered cycling down Carden Place on his way to Gordon's College when he realised that the church had been hit during the previous night's bombing raid. Being curious and knowing that no-one was likely to stop him at that hour of the morning he went into the church and found that although the east end had been wrecked, there was virtually no damage to the rest of it. The pews were in place and the hymn and prayer books seemed as though they were in place for the next service.

At the time, Prue's family did not live in Rubislaw Terrace but her parents were in the process of taking over the medical practice at No. 26, where her father had been junior partner before being called up into the RAMC. Her mother recalled that she arrived at the house to take the morning surgery to find the elderly senior partner and his house keeper struggling with a pile of debris in the centre of the hall. The debris from the "Tartan Kirkie" had flown up over the houses in Albert Terrace and a lot of it had come through the big window over the hallway at the top of the house. She promptly told Dr. Howie to take the surgery and the housekeeper to put the kettle on whilst she cleared up the mess (Prue did not know whether she recruited any patients to help with this, but would not have been surprised!) The blast had taken out some of the windows but the surgery carried on as usual. Strange to say, the magnificent mahogany banister rail and the hideous Victorian wallpaper remained unscathed. For a long time the nose cone of the bomb was used by the family as a doorstop in the surgery and remained in the house when it was later sold to an insurance company. It has since disappeared.

At the church, a special meeting was held. It was Maundy Thursday, a busy time in the church's year. The Rector, William Milne, who had only been in post a few months after the death of Canon Lightfoot, arranged 7a.m. and 8a.m. Holy Communion services for Easter Day in St. Mark's Church, Short Loanings, but wanted to hold 11am Sung Eucharist and 6.30 Evensong in nave.

Fenton Wyness, architect, was called in to inspect the damage. He reported to the vestry on 29th. April. The sanctuary, chancel, High Altar, Reredos, crypt, stonework and fabric of the organ loft, heating chamber and sacristy were a total loss. The kitchen and the main vestry were all right, except for the glass and slates. As for the nave: 'chancel arch fractured both sides, altar steps and sandstone balusters moved out of position by blast, both the North and South gables to the west of the chancel arch were cracked from the wall-head to ground level. The stonework to the rose windows in these gables had been badly shaken and slightly displaced. The West gable suffered from blast and the top stone around the rose window was in a dangerous state, having been moved fully 4"; 16 windows in the nave had been shattered and all had been shaken. The hinges of the inner door of [the] porch had been sprung. On the outside of the nave the masonry appeared to be sound except in the gables already mentioned, but several of the pinnacles and their decorative ironwork had been shaken and displaced.'

The building was declared unsafe for worship – if another bomb landed nearby it could well have collapsed. Possibilities were discussed in a general meeting of the congregation: breeze blocks were suggested to fill in the chancel arch, helped by concrete buttresses outside. One member of the congregation was determined to abandon the building altogether as it would surely be bombed again. The architect, with caution, advised that they wait a month until the building had settled further, then approach the Ministry of Supply, which controlled workmen, timber and building supplies, for material for repairs.

Meanwhile, services had to be held. Mrs. Oliver, headmistress at Albyn School, offered a free room for services. Bishop Deane (who, when he heard of the bombing, exclaimed 'Splendid! the best thing that could happen! Just what S. Mary's needs!') offered his chapel for early morning Holy Communion services.

Work begins on the ruined chancel

Salvage continued as best could be done. The remaining parts of the organ were valued at £800, the choir stalls and altar rail at £200, stored at Mr. Rattray's workshops for repair, and the fittings taken to Albyn School for the services were valued at £300. Nothing could be salvaged from the crypt until workmen were available, and the bomb crater in the crypt was liable to become waterlogged in the winter, causing a greater health hazard. Mr. Smith, jeweller, was to assess the damage to the Communion vessels. A church restoration fund was opened on 6th. May, and the response was so great in terms of letters of sympathy that a printed thank you letter was produced.

While appreciating the generosity of Albyn School and the Bishop, the Rector was eager to get the congregation back into the church. Jenkins & Marr, civil engineers, were selected to examine the church, and they declared that the nave, porch, vestry and small room adjoining the vestry could be made safe. The reopening was scheduled for October 1943, and in November the Board of Trade agreed to pay £1,145-7-4 against a claim of £1,331-0-10 for war damages, the first move in a prolonged negotiation which resulted in a slightly plainer church than F.G. Lee had built, but nevertheless a functioning church, one of only three churches in Scotland badly damaged in the air raids of the Second World War.

Probably because of the pressures of rebuilding, the matter of a war memorial was dealt with more slowly after 1946. In November 1948, the Rector suggested the grounds themselves should be a war memorial, with dignified gates. The original railings had been taken for the war effort, and would have to be replaced. Later the Rector changed his mind and suggested a communion rail for the side chapel. In the end, J. & A. Ogilvie were asked to design a rail and plaque for the war memorial, with a radiator cover for the war memorial chapel. In March 1954 £84 had been raised towards it, and it was decided to include the congregation's civilian victims. The names included on the memorial are as follows:

- Leigh Alexander No information.

- James Gillan, Flying Officer, 601 Squadron, RAF, son of William M. and Mary T. Gillan, Aberdeen. He died aged 26 on 11th. August, 1940, and is commemorated on the Runnymede memorial.

- Anthony George Lendrum Mitchell, Sergeant, 405 Squadron, RAFVR. He died on 24th. July, 1941, and is commemorated on the Runnymede Memorial.

- John Manwaring Steward Moir Sergeant, 148 Squadron, RAFVR, son of Rev George Kynoch Moir, BA, and Hilda Margaret, Hastings, Hawke Bay, New Zealand. He died aged 19 on 27th. September, 1942, and is commemorated on the Alamein Memorial.

- John Smith McKay, Flight Sergeant, 220 Squadron, RAFVR, son of John Smith McKay (commemorated on the First World War memorial) and Henrietta McKay, stepson of Mr. Marshall, vestry member, and husband of Vera Dorothy McKay, Ealing, Middlesex. He died aged 27 on 25th. October, 1943, and is commemorated on the Runnymede Memorial.

- Arthur Stanley McMaster, Private, Royal Norfolk Regiment, son of Arthur Stanley McMaster and Elizabeth Fyfe McMaster, Aberdeen. He died aged 29 on 13th. February 1942, and is buried at Kranji, Singapore.

- Alastair McKenzie Stott, Leading Aircraftman, RAFVR, son of David Stott and Jane Milne Stott, nee McKenzie. He died aged 19 on 30th March, 1941, and is buried at St. Peter's Cemetery, Aberdeen.

- James Simpson, Flight Sergeant, RAFVR, DFM, son of Mr. & Mrs. James C.T Simpson, Aberdeen. He died on 22nd September, 1942, and is buried at Springbank Cemetery, Aberdeen. 971578

- Alexander Anderson Porter, marine engineer, 60, Bedford Road, died aged 40, 21st. April, 1943

- Jessie Ann Williamina Wilson Porter, née Reid, 60, Bedford Road, died aged 41, 21st. April, 1943

- Robert Alexander Porter, engineer, 60, Bedford Road, died aged 17, 21st. April, 1943

- June Lewis Porter, 60, Bedford Road, died aged 9, 21st. April, 1943

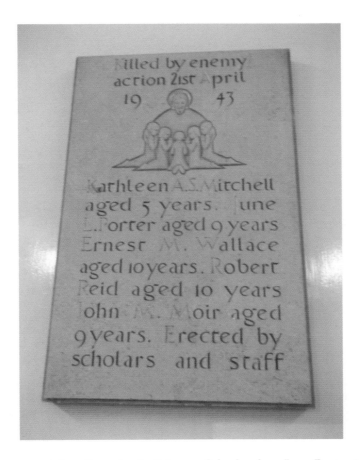

The war memorial at Sunnybank Primary School, where June Porter is also remembered, along with four other local children killed the same night.

The war and the bombing had a lasting impact on St. Mary's: gifts such as the Green Organ and the altar and triptych in the War Memorial Chapel came as a result of the restoration appeal; the dramatic photographs of the bombed church appear in many publications on wartime in Aberdeen; and still, when the wind blows in the wrong direction, dust and plaster tumble down at the east and west ends of the church, a constant memorial of the greater damage done that terrible night in 1943.

Chapter Six

Growing Up at St. Mary's, 1950s – 1970s[8]

Before the Second World War, the main children's activities at St. Mary's were the Sunday School and the League of Light Bearers, a children's organisation whose purpose was to raise money for home and foreign missions. There were Guides and Scouts in the 1920s and 1930s but they were not directly associated with the church, especially when the Scouts broke the hall windows in 1930. After the war, however, with all the challenges of the post war world, the church began to see the beginnings of the 'youth culture' that would come to fruition in the Sixties. Despite a tradition of impressive Nativity Plays (one performance was even given to Kincorth Townswomen's Guild), there were in general very few children's services, or family services: the one most likely to involve children was of course baptism.

---

[8] Most photographs in this chapter are courtesy of Malcolm Hay: the exceptions are those of the Children's Corner which comes from St. Mary's Centenary Souvenir Brochure, and the wedding photograph which appears courtesy of Anne Farquhar.

Christening of Morag Joyce Hay, 1964, with her mother Muriel and her brother Malcolm

Christening of Bruce Duncan, 1968: his brother Robert is holding him.

There were of course several children in the choir as choristers: originally it had only been boys, paid weekly according to their age, but by the 1960s girls were also members. Sometimes a child in the choir could bring a whole family into the church.

Jean Brunton and Peter Hayman, choirmaster, were married in the early 1970s and the choir formed a guard of honour on the steps. The photograph includes David Topps, Anne Pirie, Ian Webster, Cameron Pirie, Andy Pirie, Jimmy Milne, Susan McLaren, Barbara Milne and Andrew McLaren.

For part of the 1960s and 1970s the Rectory was just across the road from the church, at 17, Carden Place, and it formed a focus for church social life in a way that the church hall, far away in Rosemount, did not. The photograph of Bruce Duncan's christening above is taken on the Rectory steps, and the photograph below, on the same day in the Rectory garden.

In the Rectory garden after Bruce Duncan's christening. Included are the Rev. Thomas Turner, Margaret Murdoch, later Johnston, and Maureen Pratt. The children include Robert Duncan and Anne Pirie, later Farquhar.

The Rectory garden was the venue for church fairs and outdoor festivities, remembered with horror by Anne who had to spend one fair as a 'handkerchief girl', with handkies pinned all over her for sale! The Rectory basement was also the place for the Adventurers to meet: this was a short-lived youth association exclusive to the Scottish Episcopal Church, founded in the 1950s and all but ended by the end of the 1960s. There were no badges or uniforms like the Scouts or Boys' Brigade: it was more like a fellowship club for teenagers, with rallies on diocesan or provincial level.

An outing for the Adventurers: a brisk walk on Tullos Hill

In church on a Sunday, children were expected to keep quiet and, unless they were in the choir, not participate in the service. The children's corner proposed by Canon Milne just before the bombing was fully established, where the Green Organ is currently situated.

The Children's Corner was photographed in 1964. It was comfortably arranged for studious children with its own little altar and reading desk. The chairs and table in the above photograph are still used by children at the back of the church, and the little prie-dieu is in the Crypt.

Girls from Albyn School filed into the back pew each week in uniform. They included Gillian Hamilton, later Rose, whose children Alistair and Katie are now the fifth generation of that family to attend St. Mary's. The Albyn girls were a little detached from the children's activities at the church, having their own life at school.

However, the focus of the life of children at St. Mary's, particularly on a Sunday, was the large Sunday School.

Sunday Schools began in the 19th. century with a joint purpose: to give children a religious education (in the Episcopal Church with a view to confirmation in their teens); to give children and young people a basic education that working people might not otherwise receive; and to keep children out of mischief on the Sabbath. Sunday Schools had some traditional functions, such as the provision of a crib or an Easter garden for the church: opposite is the indoor Easter garden in the 1960s, parts of which survive today.

An outdoor garden was also prepared, at the east end of the church but not in its current position.

The Sunday School work on the Easter garden by the back wall: the spot is now planted with trees. Hats, white handbags and Sunday best, but they're still working hard!

The gardeners pose for a photograph, seated on an old pew outside the church.

None of this hard work meant that Sunday School could not be fun, too!

Once a year the Sunday School made an excursion for their picnic, often by train or specially chartered bus. In 1951, the excursion was to Ellon: this was a chance for some city children to have a rare sight of the countryside.

This cheerful bunch in their Sunday best includes, at bottom left, Muriel Lawrance, later Hay, one of the teachers.

Preparations for the Sunday School picnic were elaborate: this gentleman was the one who organised the games. His lady companion is the Aunt Sally!

Also arranged on the church steps were wooden crates of Hay's lemonade, boxes of crisps and trays of Highland toffee. But lemonade, crisps and toffees were not enough for such an expedition: one photograph shows the Mitchell & Muil bakery van providing lunch. Another shows the Grampian Transport double-decker bus chartered for the occasion.

A final photograph was taken on the church steps before the

expedition sets off. The little boy at the front is keen to be away! Included in the photograph are Anne and Cameron Pirie, Malcolm and Morag Hay and their cousin Lynn, David Topps, the Rev. William McLaren, Margaret Murdoch, and right at the edge Winnie Kerr, the Sunday School leader who took most of these pictures. She also brought along her neighbour's three boys, and many other children brought their friends.

Along with lunch there were the traditional races, running, sack, egg-and-spoon, and the competition was hot.

Parents did not escape either!

With good weather apparently guaranteed, it was a day out for the whole congregation. Here Ethel Lawrance relaxes in the sun at Torphins with a friend and a cup of tea.

The post-war world had to cater for young people in a way that the early twentieth century would hardly have recognised. The church began to look to organisations other than Sunday School, be it Light Bearers or Adventurers, to try to attract children and young adults.

The caption of this photograph reads: 'The Climax of a Diocesan Youth Festival of the Scottish Episcopal Church in Aberdeen, arrived at the finals on Friday. Bishop Hall presents Miss Muriel Lawrance with the Shield won by St. Mary's Club for the best all round performance', dated 1949.

The Sunday School picnics – and often even Sunday School classes – were somewhere you took your friends or your neighbour's children, an accepted entertainment. Today football and shopping seem to appeal more to children on a Sunday in a non-stop world: this may have been the last generation to grow up with such an acceptance of Sunday church-going and Sunday School.

Chapter Seven

The People

From its beginnings, there has been a very wide range of people associated with St. Mary's. The *Church Times* correspondent who attended a service in Correction Wynd in 1863 remarked that

> the congregation [was] composed almost entirely of the middle and poorer classes.

However, when the church moved to the new building in Carden Place, the congregation became more mixed. In this chapter there are extracts from the registers, and also more personal information about some of the clergy and laity associated with St. Mary's.

The Clergy

Much of the material in this section can be found in David Bertie's *Scottish Episcopal Clergy*.

Rev. F.G. Lee

Frederick George Lee, SCL, DCL, FSA, was born in 1832, the first son of Rev. Frederick Lee, in Thame, Oxfordshire. He attended St. Edmund's Hall, Oxford, where he won the Newdigate Prize Poem and College Prize in 1854. He briefly attended Salamanca University, Spain, and was awarded Hon DCL and FSA 1857. He became a deacon in 1854 and was ordained priest in 1856 in Oxford Diocese. He was appointed Domestic Chaplain to the Duke of Leeds and to the Earl of Morton (the father of Bishop Douglas of Aberdeen). He was curate of Sunningwell, Berkshire, from 1854 to 1856, and founder and Hon. Secretary of Association for the Promotion of the Union of Christendom, 1857-59.

He married in 1859 at Creech St. Michael, Somerset, Elvira Louisa Ostrehan, and had at least four children. Frederick Reginald Benedict Lee was baptised in July 1861 by Bishop Thomas Suther; Gordon Ambrose de Lisle Lee (named after a close colleague in the Oxford Movement and possibly Gordon of Ellon who was an early patron of St. Mary's), baptised by Rev. George Akers in August 1863, Mary, and Leonard Miles, the latter two born in London after he left

Aberdeen.

He became incumbent of St. John's, Aberdeen, in November 1859, then of St. Mary's in 1861 – 1864. In 1861, he was living in Fountain Hall, Fountainhall Road, aged 29, with his wife Elvira, aged 28, his sister Ellen Lee, two nieces and a nephew, Letitia, Maria and Robert Sewell, aged 10, 8 and 7. They had been born in the East Indies, and had presumably been sent to stay with him for their health and education, as so many children born abroad were. There were also two servants, Susan Stephen aged 21 from Aberdeen, and Jane Robertson aged 20 from Stonehaven.

> Of the Revd. Mr. Lee, John Morgan recalled: 'When I was sent on any errand to him, which was frequent, he generally appeared not at the door, like any ordinary mortal, but at one of the windows, from which he preached evasion, and illustrated the uses of procrastination to such as could not pay. Poor man, like many another, he had begun to build, without first consulting the cost and as the result showed, soon came to grief. When the work was about finished, and a good amount owing to all the Contractors as well as the Architect, our Rev. Employer became bankrupt, and took French Leave.

> *Architectural Guide to Aberdeen*

He moved to England in 1864 and became vicar of All Saints', Lambeth, Surrey, in 1867. He was received into the Roman Catholic Church in 1901. He died on 22nd. January, 1902, and is buried at Brookwood, Surrey. He was described as 'an eloquent preacher, a poet of considerable mark, an artist of no mean skill, and a heraldic student of respectable attainments.' (Gammie, 1909). His son Gordon became Bluemantle Pursuivant in the Lyon Court, following his father's interest in heraldry.

◆

Bishop Thomas Suther

Thomas George Spink Suther was born in Edinburgh in 1814 and his first incumbencies were all in Edinburgh. In 1855 he was appointed to St. Andrew's, Aberdeen, and in 1857 was elected Bishop of Aberdeen, then became Bishop of the United Diocese of Aberdeen and Orkney in 1865.

> The early years of Suther's episcopate were marked by autocracy and he clashed with several of his clergy: he suspended Rev. Patrick Cheyne of St. John's, Aberdeen, in 1858 for four years and censured Rev. James Smith of Forgue in 1859, for holding pro-Oxford Movement views. In 1862 Suther attempted to suspend Dean Wilson, incumbent of Woodhead of Fyvie, who was trying to protect the Scottish Liturgy, but this decision was overturned by the College of Bishops.
>
> Bertie

He travelled to Italy for his health in 1883, and died at San Remo, Italy, 1883.

◆

Rev. George Akers

Born in 1838 in Marylebone, London, George Akers was the sixth son of Aretas Akers, and graduated from Oriel College, Oxford, BA in 1830 and MA in 1863. He was ordained deacon in 1860 and priest the following year in Rochester Diocese, and was curate of Northfleet, Kent, from 1860 to 1862 when he moved to be curate at St. Mary's. He lived at 176, Skene Street. He seems to have left around the same time as Lee, and became a mission curate at St. Saviour's, Wellclose Square, Whitechapel, in 1864. He also later joined the Roman Catholic Church.

Rev. H.J. Palmer

Henry James Palmer was born in 1834, the fourth son of George Josiah Palmer, in Clapham, Surrey. He attended Magdalen College, Oxford, in 1854, and graduated BA from Magdalen Hall, Oxford, in 1861, and MA in 1867. He was ordained deacon in 1863 and priest in 1864 in Chester Diocese, and was both curate at Wallasey, Cheshire, and Second Master at Tower School, Liscard, Cheshire, from 1863 to 1866 when he was appointed to St. Mary's. He moved to St. Columba's, Edinburgh, in 1869, then returned to Wallasey as Headmaster of Clare Mount School in 1872.

◆

Rev. Alfred Rudall

Alfred Rudall was born in 1841, the second son of John Henry Rudall, in Kennington, Surrey. He graduated from Wadham College, Oxford, with a BA in 1865 and an MA in 1871. He was ordained deacon in 1865 in Ripon, and became curate of Christ Church, Bradford, Yorkshire. He was ordained priest in 1866 in Exeter, and was Vicar of St. Paul's, Penzance, Cornwall. He moved to St. Mary's in 1869, and while recovering from his ill-health he was chaplain to Col. Ferguson at Pitfour, before returning to Cornwall as Vicar of Carnmenellis in 1872.

◆

Rev. H.D. Jones

Henry David Jones was born in 1842 in Merthyr Tydfil, the eldest son of Robert Jones. He graduated BA from St. John's College, Cambridge, in 1865, and MA 1868. He was ordained deacon in 1865 and priest in 1866 in Yorkshire, and was curate of St. James, Kingston upon Hull, Yorkshire, from 1865 to 1867. He moved to London for a couple of years to be curate at St. Gabriel's, Pimlico, returned briefly to Wales to be curate in charge of Aberamen, Glamorgan, before moving to St. Mary's. He married Emily in 1871 and his daughter, Mary Gertrude, was baptised in St. Mary's by the Bishop in March 1872. After leaving, he became chaplain at Genoa in 1875.

◆

Rev. J.M. Danson

James Myers Danson was born in 1845 at Ingleton, Yorkshire. A graduate of Trinity College, Dublin, he was ordained deacon in 1871 and priest in 1873 in Bangor Diocese, but then taught until his first pastoral post and his marriage in 1873 to Frances Ellen Rees. He was appointed curate at St. Mary's in late 1873, and incumbent in 1874. Three of his children were baptised at St. Mary's: Arthur Llewelyn in June 1875; Edmund Wilmot in April 1877; and Mary Christabel in January 1879. He moved to Arbroath in 1880, but returned to Aberdeen in 1881 as incumbent of St. Andrew's. He was made Dean in 1907, and died in 1909. His wife died in 1932.

Rev. A.F.S. Hill

Arthur Felton Still Hill was born in 1853, and graduated BA from New College, Oxford, in 1876, and MA 1879. He also attended Lichfield Theolological College, and was ordained deacon in that diocese in 1877, though he was in York diocese when he was ordained priest in 1879. Moving again, he was curate of Handsworth, Staffordshire, from 1877 – 1879, and of St. Mary's, Hull, from 1879 to 1880, when he became incumbent of St. Mary's. His ill-health while in Aberdeen might be traced in the increasing variations in his handwriting in the registers, though he records neatly and proudly the baptism of one child in 1885 to whom he and his wife were asked to be godparents. In 1886 he became curate of St. Paul's, Clifton, Bristol, moving to St. Peter's, Harrogate, the following year. He was rector of St. John's, Maddermarket, Norwich, from 1888 to 1894, vicar of St. Bartholomew's, Lower Cam, Gloucestershire, from 1894 to 1897, and rector of Dufton, Westmoreland, from 1897 to 1905, before returning to Scotland as rector of Lasswade from 1905 to 1909, and Honorary Assistant Curate at St. Mary's Cathedral, Edinburgh, from 1909 – 1921. He died in 1936.

◆

Rev. F.W. Christie

Francis William Christie was born in Dundee in 1853, the son of James Christie. He graduated BA from St. Catherine's College, Cambridge, in 1878, and MA in 1883. He was ordained deacon in 1878 and priest in 1879, both in York Diocese. He served as curate in Penistone from 1878 to 1880, in Manchester from 1880 to 1881, and in All Saints' Helmsley, Yorkshire, from 1881 to 1886, when he moved to St. Mary's. A Canon of St. Andrew's Cathedral, he died unmarried on 15th. December, 1923, of pneumonia. He was buried in Dundee, and bequeathed to St. Mary's his vestments, small portable font and Argyll Pyx.

◆

Bishop A.G. Douglas

St. Mary's church magazine of September 1905 gave an obituary for the recently deceased Bishop Douglas, and reported on the procedures to replace him. The vestry minutes had minuted the death of Bishop Douglas in the middle of July. He had been ill for some time, but had managed to attend the laying of the foundation stone of the choir vestry at St. Mary's. He regularly visited Orkney as part of his diocesan round, and though still not well he decided to go ahead with his usual trip. Unfortunately, he was again taken ill on the journey and died in Stromness.

Arthur Gascoigne Douglas was born in 1827, the 5th. son of George Sholto Douglas, 19th. Earl of Morton. He graduated B.A. from University College, Durham, in 1849, and also attained his L.Th. and M.A. there. He was a curate in Kidderminster, then rector of St. Olave's, Southwark, and of Scaldwell, Northamptonshire, before becoming vicar of Shapwick, Dorset in 1872. In 1883 he was appointed Bishop of Aberdeen and Orkney, and his old university bestowed on him a D.D. His wife was Annamaria Richards from Wales, and his only son, Archibald, served briefly as a chaplain to the Bishop of Aberdeen. Two of his daughters were married in St. Mary's, Annie in 1887, and Ella in 1892 (she married a Church of England priest, the son of a baronet).

His funeral service took place in St. Andrew's Church, Aberdeen, five days after his death, and he was interred on the 25th. July, 1905, at Dalmahoy, near Edinburgh, where he had spent much of his childhood.

◆

Rev. H. Chapman

Henry Chapman graduated BA from Sidney Sussex College, Cambridge, in 1914, and MA in 1919, and attended Edinburgh Theological College during the First World War. He was ordained deacon in Glasgow and Galloway Diocese in 1918 and priest later the same year. He was curate at St. Mary's Cathedral, Glasgow from 1918 to 1924, in charge of St. Mathew's and St. Peter's churches. He moved to St. Mary's in 1924 at £300p.a. with the rectory. When he left in 1927, he became a vicar in Buckinghamshire.

◆

Rev. G.R. Lightfoot

George Richard Lightfoot was educated at Hatfield College, Durham, and graduated BA in 1896. He was ordained deacon in 1897 and priest the following year in the diocese of Worcester. He was curate of Oldbury, Warwickshire, from 1897, of St. Paul's, Worcester, from 1901, and of St. Peter's, Birmingham, from 1902. In 1907 he moved to Aberdeenshire to become rector of Old Deer, then of Fraserburgh from 1915 to 1927. He was made canon in 1925, and two years later moved to St. Mary's, also becoming chaplain of the House of Bethany. In 1941, his wife Edith died of lung cancer, aged 66, and he himself died the following year of cerebral embolism and coronary thrombosis, aged 70, after a short illness.

◆

Rev. W. Milne

William Milne was born in 1904 and educated at St. Paul's College, Burgh. He was ordained deacon in 1929 and priest in 1930 in the diocese of Wakefield, while he was curate of Ossett, Yorkshire. In 1932, he became priest in charge of Grantown-on-Spey (with Rothiemurchus and Kingussie), and in 1937 he was appointed priest-in-charge of Clarkston mission in Glasgow. In 1942 he moved to St. Mary's and stayed until 1965, as a canon from 1962. His last post was at Kirriemuir to 1974, but he officially retired in 1988. He was married, and his son Gavin Hall Milne, born in 1932, was city librarian, and married Elizabeth Miller, fellow library assistant at Aberdeen Public Library, in 1957.

Canon and Mrs. Milne, 1964

♦

Rev. K.E.T. Cole

Kenneth Ernest Theodore Cole, BEM 1945 (Civil), was born in 1898, and was a member of St. Mary's congregation. He acted as both rector's warden and lay reader, but in 1954 he resigned from both posts to attend Edinburgh Theological College. He was ordained deacon that year and priest the following year in the diocese of Aberdeen and Orkney, held various temporary posts, then became curate of St. Mary's in 1960. He retired in 1978, and died in 1980.

♦

Rev. T.F. Turner

Thomas Francis Turner graduated in German from Leeds University in 1950 before attending Chichester Theological College. He was ordained deacon in 1954 and priest in 1955 in Ripon Diocese, and his first three posts were all in that diocese, as curate of St. Matthew's, Holbeck, curate of St. John's, Moor Allerton, and priest in charge of St. Stephen's, Moortown, Leeds. In 1959 he became Rector of Kirkwall and Stromness, and was active in youth work, in the Scouts, Boys' Brigade and Sea Cadets. In 1965 he became Rector of St. Mary's. He left in 1968 to pursue postgraduate study at Durham University.

◆

Rev. W.H. McLaren

William Henry McLaren was born in 1927 and educated at Edinburgh Theological College. He was ordained deacon and priest in Bradford Diocese and served in that diocese until 1968, when he was appointed rector of St. Mary's. He served until 1973, when he returned to Yorkshire.

The photograph includes Harry Golding, Jean Thorburn, and brother and sister Ian and Vivian Webster.

◆

Rev. R.N. Chittenden

Roy Norman Chittenden was born in 1929 and educated at St. Chad's College, Durham, graduating B.A. in 1953. He was ordained deacon in Bath and Wells for Exeter and priest in Exeter, serving as curate at St. Thomas', Keyham, Plymouth, from 1954. His career included a period as a missionary in Nyasaland and as a teacher of religious education in several schools before he took up the incumbency of St. Mary's in 1973. He resigned in 1975.

◆

Canon J.D. Alexander

James Douglas Alexander was born in 1927 and educated at Lincoln Theological College. He was ordained deacon in 1958 and priest in 1959, both in the Diocese of Lincoln, and served first as curate of Frodingham, Scunthorpe, and then as vicar of Alvingham and rector of Keddington in Lincolnshire. He was also RAF chaplain from 1962 to 1964. After some years as rector of Gunness and Burringham, he left Lincolnshire for Aberdeen and Orkney, where he continued to serve till his retirement, first as rector of Peterhead from 1970 to 1976, with chaplaincies at Peterhead Prison and RAF Buchan, then as Rector of St. Mary's from 1976 to 1995, with chaplaincies at the Mission to Seamen, Aberdeen Port and Aberdeen Prison, as well as being priest-in-charge of St. Mary's, Cove Bay. Since his retirement, he has continued to help at St. Mary's and still attends the church.

◆

Rev. I.M. Thompson

Ian Malcolm Thompson was educated in London and Aberdeen, graduating B.Th. in 1998. He was a Salvation Army officer from 1979 to 1993, but was ordained deacon in 1994, and priest in 1995. He became Bishop's Chaplain at Old Deer, Longside and Strichen from 1994 to 1996, and Rector of St. Mary's from 1996 to 1999, and at the same time served as Diocesan Youth Chaplain and Provincial Youth Co-ordinator. In 1999, he moved to take up the post of Chaplain and Dean of Selwyn College, Cambridge. Ian Thompson was the instigator of the link with our sister church of St. Mary's, Diss, Norfolk, where his parents worshipped.

◆

Rev. Clive Clapson

Clive Henry Clapson was born in 1955. He graduated BA from Leeds University in 1976, and M.Div. from Trinity College, Toronto, in 1979. He was ordained deacon in 1979 and priest in 1980 in the Diocese of Ontario, and served as curate at St. Thomas', Belleville, 1979 – 1980, and as rector of Loughborough, 1980 to 1983, both in that diocese. In 1983 he moved to California and was vicar of Christ the King Mission, Alpine, San Diego, till 1988, when he moved again to England. He served as curate at Hawley Green, Guildford, till 1990, then as Rector of Invergordon till 2000. He was Rector of St. Mary's from 2000 to 2005, when he moved to St. Salvador's, Dundee.

The Congregation

In November 1865, the following were the constituent members of the congregation:

Thomas Gordon Beveridge
George Bruce
Joseph Cumine senior
Joseph Cumine junior
William Cumming
Rev. T.D. Dove
George Forbes
Alexander Fraser senior

Alexander Fraser junior
Francis Fraser
James Fraser
John Fraser senior, organist
John Fraser junior
William Fraser senior
William Fraser junior
William McKessock
Farquhar Mathieson
George Matthew
George Milne
James Nicol
George Oldman junior
Alexander Sangster junior
Alexander Smith
Charles Smith
William Tyson, clerk
Thomas Watt

In April, 1877, the vestry were scattered about the grander and less grand parts of the town:

Rev. J.M. Danson 7, Waverly Place
John Coleman, 81, Wales Street
Alexander Fraser,   57, Green
R.B. Horne 8, Queen's Terrace
John Hunter 20, Upper Denburn
John Keith 7, Bonaccord Square
John Ligertwood 36, Bonaccord Terrace
Dr. Smith-Shand 256, Union Street
John White 18, Whitehouse Street.

In 1890 women members of the congregation were allowed to vote for the first time, though Miss Urquhart had been on the finance committee since 1885.

From the Baptism Registers:

The baptisms registered at St. Mary's Temporary Chapel are all marked 'conditionally', presumably without the licence of the Bishop. Most happened at the chapel, but some were carried out at the child's home (particularly if it was ill) and one or two were carried out at Lee's home.

The first baptism in the new church was that of Alexander Thomas Gordon Beveridge, son of Thomas Gordon Beveridge, church warden, and his wife Agnes, of Mount St. Ternan, Banchory. It took place on 3rd. April, 1864, only a few days after St. Mary's opened as a proprietary chapel.

In the 1860s, baptisms came thick and fast: there were six on the 2nd. May, 1865, and another six the following Sunday. There is an air almost of a personality cult about the church: more than half of the early baptisms are of adults or much older children.

'Riddell, Elizabeth (a child about whose parentage I can learn nothing), aged 14, was baptised by me in church Feb. 15th., 1880'.

There was a trend for naming children after the incumbent – in full. Henry James Palmer Smith was baptised in December 1881 and James Myers Danson Milne in May of that year, both by A.F.S. Hill. George Akers, the curate, baptised Frederick George Lee Wall and George Akers Taylor in the 1860s.

From the Marriage Registers:

The first marriage recorded in the registers is on 17th. February, 1862, 'at the temporary church of St. Mary'. The couple were Alexander Milne, seaman, and Elizabeth Moore Falconer.

The couples marrying were generally from humbler addresses at this time, Ship Row, Gallowgate, etc., until Mathew Owen Coleman, MB, and 'Elizabeth Jamieson daughter of a shipowner' married in November 1869.

Every trade seems to have been represented in those marrying at St. Mary's: the registers record pedlars, omnibus conductors, poultry maids, doctors, radiographers, clerkesses, tea planters, papermill workers, university lecturers, gentry, fish friers, and envelope workers.

In 1896, H.J.G. Grierson, Professor of English Literature, married Mary Letitia Ogston, daughter of Professor Alexander Ogston of Surgery (of Soapy Ogston's family).

In 1888 Charles Allan Logan, 51, a widower, married his servant Isabella Milne, aged 33.

A television technical assistant and a radio and television salesman both married in 1957, and in 1963 Wilhelm Karl Hermanns, headwaiter, and Marjorie Jay West, hotel receptionist, married, both employed at the Marcliffe, Queen's Terrace. The same year Henry Alexander William Baird of Durris House married the local schoolteacher, Alison Mary Barlas.

The arts were represented, too: Christina Evelyn Brown, operatic singer, married draper's warehouseman Arthur Beattie in 1909, and Allan MacArthur, journalist, married Rose Charlotte Winter, artist, in 1920.

Though there was less sign of it during the course of the First World War, there was a little flood of servicemen marrying in 1918 and 1919. In the Second World War there were many service people marrying in St. Mary's, with both their service title and their trade noted, from all over UK. As late as 1963 the Rector was marrying RAF Corporal Richard King and WRAF SAW Irene Smith. There was a wedding in church as early as 28th. December, 1943, after the bombing.

Not every marriage was a success, of course, but one dramatic end is recorded in the register: James Phillips baker, bachelor, 19 Marywell Street and Margaret Thompson, spinster, general servant, 3, Queen's Cross, married 10th. April, 1876. A note is added: '(This marriage is annulled by the fact of Margaret Thompson's having been proved to have a husband still alive.)'.

From the Burial Registers:

Archibald Reith married Mary Bisset on 2nd. December, 1882. He was 28, she was 22, and their parents (his father was a police sergeant and hers was a market gardener) were all dead by then. They lived at 28, Skene Row, but by 1889 they had moved to 155, Hardgate. Archibald was a linen bleacher and suffered from heart disease, and he died and was buried on 6th. August in Nellfield Cemetery. Mary was left with a baby, also Archibald, possibly born after his father's death. Young Archibald never thrived, and he died at fourteen days old. He was buried at Nellfield ten days after his father. It's likely that their accommodation was not healthy, anyway: on 18th. October Mary herself was buried in Nellfield, dead at the age of 29 from phthisis pulmonum, or as we would call it, tuberculosis.

David Warrack aged 26, leading seaman on HMS Collingwood, was buried at Nellfield on 6th. May, 1896. 'Service at the house; body borne by men from HM Training Ship Clyde, firing party at grave.' Despite this grand send-off, David had not died in conflict, but of intestinal ulceration and peritonitis.

Alice Lydia Ollis was aged 35 when she died in 1896, of pneumonia and premature accouchement. She was the wife of Hugh Gourlay, an early telephone engineer, who lived at 89, Claremont Street. He himself died very suddenly six months later, also aged 35, of gastritis syncope.

'Jackson, Jane (a coloured woman born in Jamaica) was buried by me in the Cathedral Churchyard of St. Machar May 18th. 1875'. She was a domestic servant, who died of old age in the Oldmachar Poorhouse – aged only fifty.

George Milne, City Chamberlain and church warden, died in 1876 aged 52.

Joseph Holmes, formerly butler to Cunliffe Brooks, the eccentric owner of the Glentanar Estate, died aged 52, and was buried 15th. February, 1890.

Thomas John Bremner of Haddo-Rattray and Glasslaw, 42, Carden Place, aged 79, was buried in St. Nicholas' Kirkyard in 1890. He was a long-term supporter of St. Mary's, and after his death crystal cruets were presented in his memory.

Three of the children of John Gordon of Cairnbulg belonged to St. Mary's: Sarah Janet Gordon, his eldest daughter, died in March 1893, aged 79; his third son, Alexander Crombie Gordon, Vice-Admiral, 3 Albyn Place, died in 1894, aged 75; his youngest daughter, Catherine Erskine Gordon, Mormond Lodge, Murtle, died aged 72 in May 1900. They were all buried in Rathen kirkyard. John Gordon of Cairnbulg was at the meeting appointing F.G. Lee as Rector of St. John's in 1860.

St. Mary's Connexions

Professor Smith-Shand

One of the early vestry members (he appears on the 1877 list) was Dr. James Smith, who later adopted his first wife's surname along with his own and became Smith-Shand. She was Barbara Sangster Sharp Shand: after her death he married Anna Stuart. He attended most vestry meetings despite an increasing workload in general practice and in teaching at the university, and was a very active member of the church in the diocese. He was appointed Regius Professor of the Practice of Medicine, but died suddenly at his home, 17, Albyn Place, of a cerebral haemorrhage, aged 57. His funeral took place on 16th. June, 1891, and was attended by the Bishop, many other clergy, the Principal of the University, other professors, and many doctors, amounting to 200 – 300 mourners, who formed a cortege from St. Mary's, where the funeral service was held, to St. Machar's kirkyard, where he was buried near the side gate against the wall.

The Disney Leiths

Mary Charlotte Julia Gordon, daughter of Sir Henry Gordon of Knockespoch, married Robert William Disney Leith (1819–1892) in 1865. He was a general who had lost his arm at the Battle of Mooltan. She was already a published writer of children's fiction but also of translations from the Icelandic and later memoirs of travels to Iceland: she bathed in the sea on the coast of Iceland when she was seventy! She was a cousin of the poet A. C. Swinburne (1837–1909), and also wrote adult fiction. She died in 1926 at the age of 86, at her family home in the Isle of Wight. Her obituary in the *Glasgow Herald* states:

> From early days Mrs. Disney Leith made Church music a serious study. At Northcote she acted as long as health would permit as organist at her parish church, following a tradition established by her father.

She was also organist at St. Drostan's, Insch, and previously of St. Mary's, Inverurie, Aberdeenshire.

Alexander Henry, son of Mary and Robert Disney Leith, was born on 27th. July, 1866, and baptised the following month. His sister Mary Levina was born and baptised in 1867. The family lived at 49, Victoria Street. Mary Gordon's grandfather was Sir William Gordon of Oyne, for whom the Green Organ was built (see The Music): Mary Levina was the lady who gifted the Green Organ to St. Mary's after the bombing.

The Mintos

William Minto was born in Alford, Aberdeenshire, in 1845, and educated at Aberdeen University. He was assistant to Professor Alexander Bain at Aberdeen and made a study of English Literature. Moving to London in 1873, he contributed journalistic articles on politics and literary criticism and wrote for the *Encyclopaedia Britannica*, as well as completing three novels. In early 1880 he married Cornelia Beatrice Griffiths, daughter of an English rector, and moved back to Aberdeen to take Bain's place in the chair of Logic and English. He and his wife had at least two children: William Griffiths Bain Minto was born at 8, Westfield Terrace, Aberdeen, on 13th. November 1880, and Cornelia Grace Frances Minto was baptised in St. Mary's on 19th. September 1884. Minto died of tuberculosis in 1892. Two years later, Cornelia married Williamson Booth, a solicitor in Aberdeen, son of a doctor. Sadly she died in childbirth in January 1896, aged 33. Her son William died at the end of the First World War (see *Wartime*). The family were involved with the work of the House of Bethany, the Episcopalian convent in the west end, and it was there they met a local poet, Elizabeth Craigmyle, who had wandered from the Church of Scotland through atheism to Episcopalianism, influenced by the sisters there. When William Minto died, she published a poem in his memory in the *Aberdeen University Review*[9].

---

[9] *Aberdeen University Review*, Vol. VII, No. 20, March 1920.

On the Evening of a Funeral

'Peace hath her victories as renowned as War.'
Peace hath her sombre tragedy as well:
He bore a charmed life through the shot and shell,
Gallant and gay, insouciant; not a scar,
('Not even a scratch!' said laughingly,) when afar
He fought, and now some hideous miracle
Has brought an end like this, - the passing bell,
The men he loved following a flag-draped car.

Strange silly trifles come from memory's store,
As I recall a schoolboy's bright, brown eyes,
Evenings with story-books, stamps, butterflies,
And far, far off – O weird, impossible thing!
(Not for the soldier is my heart so sore)
A little child that used to kiss and cling.

The Lumsdens

Clements Lumsden, son of Harry, was an advocate in Aberdeen, 1796 – 1853 (his grave is in St. Nicholas' Kirkyard near the gate to Church Lane). He married Jane, third daughter of James Forbes of Echt, a forthright woman whose diary was later published by her daughter. They had five daughters, three of whom were remarkably influential women: Katharine Maria was honorary superintendent (that is, matron) of the Royal Hospital for Sick Children, and her younger sister Rachel Frances was in turn matron of the Children's Hospital and then of the Royal Infirmary. Louisa Innes, the youngest sister, was one of the first five students at Girton College, Cambridge, the first female students in the United Kingdom. She went on to lecture in classics at Girton, and was the first headmistress of St. Leonard's School, St. Andrews – she is also credited with introducing lacrosse to British schools! She was made a Dame for her contribution to education. These impressive women had two brothers, Henry William and James Forbes. James Forbes Lumsden's youngest child, Helen Amy, was baptised in St. Mary's by the Bishop on 26th. June, 1881. Their coachman, William Henry Croft, and their cook, Rose Alexander, were married in St. Mary's in 1891, giving their address as Johnston House, Rubislaw, the Lumsdens' town house.

The Mackinnons

The Mackinnon name is a well-known one in the Aberdeen Society of Advocates. There have been at least four La(u)chlan Mackinnons, and other sons were also advocates. The Lachlan Mackinnon born in 1886 was married in 1914 to Marjory, daughter of Robertson Barclay Gordon, Procurator Fiscal of Elginshire. He served with the Gordon Highlanders during the First World War and was taken prisoner with his battalion. His mother Theodora set up a splendid prisoner-of-war support society, sending food parcels and supplies to all Gordon Highlander prisoners in Germany, a society that was expanded to include other servicemen until the process was eventually taken over by the Red Cross. Lachlan and Marjory had a son who was named Lachlan: rebelling against the family tradition, he became a schoolmaster, and married in St. Mary's in 1955.

Celebrity Burns Supper

A Burns Supper was planned in 1959 for 1960 to which Lord and Lady Tweedsmuir and Hector Hughes were to be invited as guest speakers – rather different from today's informal affairs!

Trustees

The Trustees were all men of note in the Aberdeen Diocese.

Hon George Frederick Boyle of Cumbrae, 1825 – 1890, later Earl of Glasgow, was founder of Cumbrae College and collegiate church, now the Cathedral for the Isles.

John Ramsay of Barra in Aberdeenshire, 1831 – 1895, was the

son of John Ramsay of Barra and Susan Innes, daughter of Alexander Innes of Pitmedden. He married Leonora Bond, daughter of a clergyman, and had two daughters, one of whom married Francis Irvine of Drum.

> Another visitor to Barra in the late 1930s was the Bishop of Aberdeen and Orkney, who was intrigued during one visit by the sight of a monkey larking about in a tree. He told his hosts that he was struck by the monkey's resemblance to Sandy Macpherson, one of his clergymen, and thereafter the animal was known by that name.
>
> *The Leopard,* April 2008

George Auldjo Jamieson, 1828 – 1900, was a noted accountant and businessman, based in Edinburgh, but from Aberdeen and with many North-East connexions.

Alexander Forbes Irvine of Drum, 22nd. Laird, died in 1922. The Irvine family has had a long association with the Episcopal Church and with the law.

Norval Clyne was born at Ballycastle in 1817, and became an advocate in Aberdeen. He was a leading member of the congregation at St. John's, Crown Terrace, when Rev. F.G. Lee resigned, and later became a trustee of St. Mary's. Around 1860, he and his fellow St. John's member and advocate, George Grubb, led a petition to Bishop Suther and the Diocesan Synod, 'pointing out the deficiencies of "due and legitimate provision for the co-operation of the laity in connection with the administration of the affairs of the Church", and requesting the Synod to consider admitting the laity to share in church administration'[10]. His family were intimately associated with the Scottish Episcopal Church: his second daughter, Lizzie Mary, married John Skinner Wilson, the rector of Woodhead of Fyvie, and his fourth daughter, Edith Angela, married the Rev. Robert Cruickshank, rector of St. John's, Crown Terrace. His fourth son, Arthur Clyne, was the noted architect who made many contributions to both exterior and interior of St. Mary's, designing the Choir Vestry and the pulpit. Norval Clyne died in January, 1889.

---

[10] NRA(S) 2698: Records of the Cathedral Church of St. Andrew, Aberdeen.

.

Chapter Eight

St. Mary's Today

The Reverend Canon Graham Smith Taylor is the current Rector of St Mary's Episcopal Church, Carden Place, Aberdeen.

Graham was born and raised in Buckie on the Moray coast. After having worked in retail management, he entered the ministry of the Scottish Episcopal Church in 1998 firstly with the Theological Institute for training. He was then ordained Deacon in 2001 then Priest in 2002 serving his title at St Mary-on-the-Rock, Ellon with St James the Less, Cruden Bay with specific responsibility for St Peter's, Peterhead. During the years 2004-2005 he became the Priest in Charge of St Peter's and Associate Priest of St Mary-on-the-Rock and St James the Less.

In 2005, Graham became the Rector of St Mary's, Carden Place, Aberdeen and in 2006 he was appointed the Diocesan Director of Ordinands. In 2008, he was made a Canon of St Andrews Cathedral, Aberdeen. From 2009 – 2012, in addition to his other responsibilities, Graham became Rector of St Clement's, Mastrick, Aberdeen with oversight of the Curate and congregation.

Since September, 2013, Graham has been Episcopal Hospital Chaplain for Aberdeen Hospitals. He is assisted at St. Mary's by the Rev. Jason Hobbs, Assistant Priest.

Jason adds: 'I was born in County Durham in 1974 and spent

a very happy eighteen years living there with my parents and younger brother. My first degree was in applied chemistry and lead on to a year working as an analytical chemistry. I decided that was not the life for me and retrained as a secondary music teacher. I moved to Aberdeen in 2001 and worked at Oakbank school for 4 years. I then began working at Hazlehead Academy as a SFL teacher and became head of department in 2012. While still teaching I completed my ministerial training at TISEC and became curate at St Mary's in 2010. I am now the assistant priest working alongside Canon Graham Taylor. I feel privileged to serve such a very special congregation and look forward to many happy years at Carden Place.'

The vestry at the time of the anniversary of the opening of the Carden Place church are:

> Rector's Warden: David Rose
> People's Warden: Rachael Cormack
> Secretary: Mary Allardyce
> Treasurer: Lydia Ross
> Lay Representative: Nicola Mills
> Ordinary Vestry Members: Dave Dillard, Freddie Stephens, Simon Rosario, Jenny Cruickshank, Margaret MacKinnon and David Brown.

The congregation numbers around 160 and draws its members, as always, from all over Aberdeen and all kinds of background.

Worship

The regular weekly services in 2014 are:

Sunday: Holy Eucharist at 8a.m. and 10.15a.m., with the 10.15 service alternating between the 1970 and 1982 liturgies.

Tuesday:
Morning Prayer at 7.45a.m.

Wednesday:
Holy Eucharist at 10a.m.

Thursday:
Morning Prayer at 7.45a.m.

In addition to these weekly services, the church is open each Friday at lunchtime for anyone wishing to visit, pray or talk. On the last Tuesday of the month, there is a short lunchtime service aimed generally to the office workers around the church, for in contrast to the comfortable residential area which grew up round the church in the early twentieth century, many of the nearby houses are now offices for oil companies and accountants. St. Mary's has also led a trend in the Diocese for Healing services: on the first Sunday of the month there is an evening service of healing, and prayers for healing also take place after the 10.15 Sunday service in the War Memorial Chapel for anyone in need.

There is a quietly active Prayer Group meeting weekly. Sunday School is still in existence, though after a period of having many children in church the congregation is now a little short of children.

Partnerships and Outreach:

St. Mary's is part of the Diocese of Aberdeen and Orkney of the Scottish Episcopal Church, which is a member of the Anglican Communion. The S.E.C. is also part of the Porvoo Agreement with churches in northern Europe and the E.M.U. Members of St. Mary's congregation include the Diocesan Communications Officer, the Honorary Diocesan Archivist, and three of the Diocesan representatives on the Provincial Synod.

St. Mary's has two sister churches, one at St. Mary's, Diss, in Norfolk, and the other at St. Mary's, Mqanduli, in the Anglican Diocese of Mthatha in South Africa. In 2012 St. Mary's invited the Rev. Mlu Mbele, then Rector of St. Mary's Mqanduli, to visit Aberdeen with his family.

Locally, St. Mary's shares services and social activities with several neighbouring churches of various denominations.

Rev. Mlu Mbele with Rev. Graham Taylor

The Diocese of Mthatha (previously St. John's, Transvaal) is twinned with the Diocese of Aberdeen and Orkney. St. Mary's also has close links with St. Clement's in Mastrick, Aberdeen.

The congregation regularly supports Barnardo's, Aberlour Children's Charity, Christian Aid and Missions to Seafarers, amongst other charities.

Other Activities

A monthly Music Cafe takes place in the church to benefit from the splendid acoustics. Young adults meet for prayer and socialising in the LEGO group. There are now teams to support the Rector in pastoral work, to arrange fund-raising activities, and to deal with information and communication: the church is currently enjoying its third website. In contrast to the early days of St. Mary's, the church is cleaned weekly by members of the congregation. There are many social events, including barbecues, wine tastings, silent auctions, carol singing, Easter breakfasts, and bring and share lunches. There is a busy Fair Trade stall, and the church has participated in the City's Doors Open Day.

In today's steady and 'middle church' congregation, the Rev. Frederick Lee might find difficulty in recognising the St. Mary's he founded. Vestments and decorations can be found all over the Scottish Episcopal Church, but incense is rarely used in Carden Place. There are more women on the vestry than men, and we have had a woman curate. The debt is clear, though it is always a challenge to maintain an old building and carry out our mission in today's more secular age. But it is a rare person today who would attend the Sunday morning service and leave before the Eucharist, and that, at least, would please Mr. Lee!

St. Mary's and the B.B.C.

The Green Organ has made at least two appearances on the Home Service, both in the 1950s, and other organ recitals and services have been broadcast, including one featuring the schoolgirl flautist, Ann Lennox. However, a more unusual connexion was on *Mastermind* in the early 2000s: the specialist subject was Aberdeen Architecture, and the question? 'What is the nickname of the unusual church dedicated to St. Mary in Aberdeen's Carden Place?' The answer, of course: 'The Tartan Kirkie'.

References:

Aberdeen City Archives, Old Aberdeen House, Dunbar Street, Aberdeen:

DD321 Records of St. Mary's Episcopal Church, Carden Place
DD540 Records of St. John's Episcopal Church, Crown Terrace

Aberdeen University Archives, Duncan Rice Library, Aberdeen:

MS3759 William Douglas Simpson collection of archaeological, monumental and architectural plans

Publications:

Bailey, Rebecca M.: *Scottish Architects' Papers*, Edinburgh 1996
Bertie, David: *Scottish Episcopal Clergy*, London 2000
Brogden, W.A.: *An Illustrated Architectural Guide to Aberdeen*, Edinburgh 1998
Gammie, Alexander: *The Churches of Aberdeen, historical and descriptive*, Aberdeen 1909

ABOUT THE AUTHOR

N.J. Mills is a freelance archivist based in Aberdeen and has been Lay Representative of St. Mary's for twelve years.

Made in the USA
Columbia, SC
26 February 2018